The
OTHER
FACES *of*
MARY

The OTHER FACES *of* MARY

STORIES, DEVOTIONS, AND PICTURES OF THE HOLY VIRGIN AROUND THE WORLD

ANN BALL

A Crossroad Book
The Crossroad Publishing Company
New York

The Crossroad Publishing Company
481 Eighth Avenue, New York, NY 10001

Unless otherwise noted, all art is credited to the local informant mentioned in the relevant chapter.

Additional information about the images of Mary in this book can be found in the special section "Other Faces of Mary" on the author's website: www.annball.com.

This book is set in 11/13 AGaramond.
The display type is AGaramond with AGaramond Alt initial letters.

Printed in the United States of America

Library of Congress Cataloging-in-Publication Data

Ball, Ann.
    The other faces of Mary : stories, devotions, and pictures of the
Holy Virgin around the world / Ann Ball.
        p. cm.
    Includes bibliographical references.
    ISBN 0-8245-2255-9 (alk. paper)
    1. Mary, Blessed Virgin, Saint—Devotion to. I. Title.
BT645.B32 2005
232.91—dc22
                                                        2004023076

1   2   3   4   5   6   7   8   9   10   08   07   06   05   04

Contents

Preface

We are familiar with many of the great titles of Mary, such as Our Lady of Lourdes, Our Lady of Fatima, and Our Lady of Guadalupe, but there are other faces of Mary that, although less known and often honored only locally, vividly point out the universal love of Our Lady for and by all nations. Although specific to a certain time and place, these devotions, no matter how ancient, have a striking relevance for Christians today. By looking at the other faces of Mary, we see reflected the twin jewels of the cultural diversity and universal sameness of the Catholic faith.

> For many and many a time, in grief,
> My weary fingers wandered round
> Thy circled chain, and always found
> In some Hail Mary sweet relief.
> —from Rev. Abram J. Ryan, "My Beads" (ca. 1882)

This book is written for my children, as always, and especially for my friend Pat, who loves Mary.

The image of Our Lady of Harissa looks down on her devotees at the National Shrine of Our Lady of Lebanon, in North Jackson, Ohio.

Introduction

In the Christmas carol "Some Children See Him," the author, Willa Hutson, makes the point that children throughout the world see the Christ Child in different ways: some see him lily white; some see him bronzed and brown; some see him almond eyed. She concludes that throughout the world, people see the Baby Jesus' face like their own, "but bright with heav'nly grace," and she calls all to bring their hearts in offering to the Love born on Christmas night.

What is true of Christ is also true of Mary. She has transcended every culture and ethnic group, and like our Holy Father and the Catholic Church herself, she is universal.

In the first century of the Christian era, Mary appeared to the discouraged apostle James while he was in Spain. She appeared there on a pillar; the apostle then regained his strength and continued his missionary journey. Many women since then carry the Spanish name Pilar, in honor of that appearance.

More than 1,400 years later, and after many other appearances, Mary appeared to a Mexican peasant, Juan Diego. Although Spaniards brought Christianity to the New World, Mary appeared not as a Spanish noblewoman but as an Aztec peasant woman, an amazing image that took the New World by surprise and even imprinted itself on the *tilma* (cloak) of an astonished Juan Diego—complete with the reflection of an awe-struck Juan Diego in the pupils of her eyes. Mary was pregnant and was adorned with the traditional Aztec cultural sign for pregnancy, a delicate ribbon laced over her stomach. Mary of Guadalupe honored the Aztec culture; but instead of glorifying its ritual of human sacrifice to Aztec gods, Mary honored the child in her womb. A new dawn appeared in the New World, and Mary's message still resounds today that children are gifts to be reverenced, even and especially in their mother's womb.

Five hundred years later, Mary appeared in a field near Fatima, Portugal, to three small children. She left them with prophecies, concerns, and warnings that helped shape Catholic life in the twentieth century, finding completion only in the revelation and explanation of the "third secret" in the jubilee year 2000. How amazing are these warnings and how insightful were they with regard to the threats to human society of that century, called humanity's "dark night of the soul."

One also sees images of Mary throughout Lebanon, a land that Pope John Paul II recognized with its very own synod of bishops, and one that the Holy Father has said is "more than a country, a message of conviviality for the world." With its mixture of Christians and Muslims, Lebanon is a paradigm for our present world. With divine assistance, Mary's prayer, and the good will of her people, Lebanon may be proof that the "clash of cultures" is not our doomed destiny. Rather, Muslims, Christians, and Jews share a common destiny, and Mary is for all of us a common bond. Mary is found in every chapel, roadside shrine, and mountaintop of Christian Lebanon; and she is revered there also by her Muslim compatriots. Her image graces the Bay of Jouneih on the top of the hill of Harissa. Mary, for Middle Eastern Christians, is a special grace and friend, as she had been in every generation and every culture and every nation where the gospel message has lived under precarious and fragile support from the world.

My involvement in this beautiful work of Ann Ball, which was undertaken to show the "other faces of Mary that, although less known and often honored only locally, vividly point out the universal love of Our Lady for and by all nations," came through a series of e-mails. She was looking for help with her chapter on Our Lady of Lebanon, a request that I was only too happy to accommodate. In the midst of this correspondence I received a call from the Maronite patriarch in Lebanon that would forever change my life. He asked if I would accept the nomination of the

Maronite Synod of Bishops, confirmed by the Holy Father and the Holy See, to become third bishop of the eparchy (diocese) of St. Maron of Brooklyn, New York.

I continued to assist Ann during this entire process until my cover was blown, and she discovered that "Father" Gregory was actually "Bishop-elect" Gregory. In gratitude for my assistance and in her desire to show the many faces of Mary in every culture and ethnic group, Ann asked if I would write a brief introduction to this present work.

Like Mary who appeared to St. James in Spain as Our Lady of the Pillar, to Juan Diego as Our Lady of Guadalupe, to the shepherd children as Our Lady of Fatima, and to Christians in the Middle East as Our Lady of Lebanon, Mary continues in our day as the special intercessor and helper of Christians who invoke her help. She is for us a Mother who makes each of her children feel that she is there for us alone. She, like her Divine Son, is truly *for us and for our salvation.*

I hope that this book will give the reader another glance at Mary, Mother of Jesus, Mother of God, and our Mother as well, a glance seen through the eyes of those who looked for her assistance through their own eyes and their own needs.

Mary, Help of Christians and of all who seek her intercession, pray for us.

Gregory John Mansour
Bishop of the Eparchy
of St. Maron of Brooklyn

This painting depicts the nativity of Mary, an unusual image in art. St. Joachim prays in the foreground as St. Anne rests in bed.

The Nativity of Mary

Maria Bambina
Italy–United States

Images of both the Infant Jesus and the baby Mary were popular objects of veneration throughout Europe during the eighteenth century. In Milan, Italy, there is an statue of Mary, made of wax, known as the *Maria Bambina*.

The life-size, realistic image was made about 1735 by a Poor Clare nun in Todi and brought to Milan in 1738 by Bishop Alberico Simonetta. After his death, the image was given to the Capuchin sisters. In 1810, during the reign of Emperor Joseph II, religious orders were suppressed, but the little image was kept safe by one of the sisters. It was eventually passed to the pastor of St. Marco Church, who gave it to the Sisters of Charity of Lovere. They took it with them when they assumed the direction of the Ciceri Hospital in 1842. In 1876, it was moved to its current location at the sisters' motherhouse, where it was placed in the novitiate.

During the octave of the Nativity of Mary, the baby was moved to the chapel in celebration of the feast. With the passage of time, the image had become dirty and discolored, so eventually it was taken from the novitiate and put away in storage. It was brought out for veneration only during the octave.

On the feast of the Nativity in September of 1884, one of the sisters begged the superior to bring the little image of Maria Bambina to the infirmary and to let it remain with her during the night. On the following morning, the superior was inspired to take the image around to the other sick sisters. A devout novice took the little Bambina in her arms and begged her for the return of her health. Immediately, she was miraculously cured of a crippling paralysis. Two of the other sisters in the infirmary were also cured.

In October, the statue was given new clothing and placed in a beautiful cradle in a temporary chapel. Only the face is seen; she is wrapped in "swaddling" clothes, in the style of the Middle Ages. Infants were wrapped in swaddling clothes and bound tightly to ensure that their limbs grew straight.

The sisters began to venerate the image and request favors, and the Bambina answered their pleas. By January of the following year, an amazing and inexplicable transformation began to occur. The faded gray complexion of the image slowly changed to warm flesh tones, which made the statue seem almost alive and gave it the appearance of a living baby. Soon, people from the city heard of the miracle, and they began to come to venerate the miraculous image. A new chapel, open to the public, was dedicated in 1888.

Maria Bambina was solemnly crowned by Cardinal Ferrari in 1904, and in 1909 devotion to Maria Bambina was enriched with indulgences by Pope St. Pius X.

As the devotion spread throughout Italy, an archconfraternity and a League of the Innocent were formed. A small wax copy of the image became a popular wedding gift. The small images are still made today, although few of the younger sisters know the ancient art of working in wax.

The shrine and the motherhouse were destroyed by bombing during World War II, but the image had been taken to safety. It remained in the temporary motherhouse of the sisters until the new motherhouse and shrine were built in 1953. Annually, on September 8, the sisters touch the image with small pieces of cotton, which are distributed as sacramentals. Today, numerous supplicants come to bring their petitions to Maria Bambina. Young couples who want the gift of a child are among the most fervent of her devotees. Many return, holding their newborns, to thank her for prayers answered.

Devotion to Maria Bambina has spread throughout the world. For many years, an image of Maria Bambina was on display in a niche in the altar of the crypt of St. Anne's Church in Jerusalem. Although a small chapel was built over the grotto during the second century, the first church was built there in the last part of the fifth century. It is the fifth Christian church built in Jerusalem. In the eleventh century, the church was destroyed; the current church was rebuilt in the twelfth century by the crusaders. In 1192, Salah Ed Din turned this new church into a *madrasah* (school of Quranic law), and it thereby repeatedly escaped destruction. It was not until 1856, however, that it became a Christian shrine again. In gratitude for the help given to Turkey by the French Government, Sultan Abdoul Majid presented the church to Emperor Napoleon III. Since 1878, the Missionaries of Africa have been the guardian of this shrine, which tradition holds marks the spot of the Virgin's birth. The cave was initially marked off by the crusaders, who followed the Eastern tradition that Mary was born in Jerusalem near the pool of Bethesda.

The crypt is reached by descending a broad flight of steps to a tiny chapel with a domed ceiling. Here there is an altar dedicated to the birth of Our Lady. The setting for the altar is about six feet square. Above the altar stands a small statue of Mary, and paintings of Sts. Anne and Joachim flank it on either side. An image of the infant Mary rested in a small recess sculpted from the stone of the altar table. Unfortunately, at one time the original image was refurbished, but the job was so poorly done that the image was removed. One of the congregations of Sisters of the Infant Jesus offered a replacement wax image, but this was later moved to the chapel of the Italian hospital in Nazareth.

Although devotion to the infant Mary is still little known in the United States, that may be changing. Among her other advocations, Maria Bambina is seen by many as a wonderful advocate for the respect for life.

Sister Mary Lawrence Scanlan, a member of the Franciscan Sisters of Allegany, has always had a strong devotion to the childhood of Mary. In the late 1950s, she was appointed vocation director of her order and was inspired to write a little chaplet in the Virgin's honor, called the "Garland of the Holy Child Mary." In the late 1950s, her community began to disseminate leaflets of the Garland for the intention of obtaining vocations to the priesthood and the religious life.

Sister Mary Lawrence was delighted when her long-time friend Fr. Benedict Ballou, O.F.M., brought her from Italy a replica of the Maria Bambina of Milan. The beautiful image was placed in the novitiate, where it remained for many years. The chaplet spread to many of the laity who came in contact with the sisters. Devotion to the image of the Bambina, however, remained with the novices of the congregation. Once, however, they loaned their little Bambina to the Cloistered Dominicans, whose monastery was near their hospital in Camden, New Jersey. The nuns had asked to borrow it for their celebration of the feast in honor of Mary's birthday. When the novitiate was moved from the motherhouse, the little image remained for a time in the room of the novice mistress. When the novice mistress died, the statue was placed in the archives of the congregation, where it remained for a number of years. Today, the image is venerated in the Sacred Heart Oratory.

Another person who has a deep devotion to the baby Mary is Father Donald Noiseux. Nearly twenty-five years ago, in preparing to enter the seminary, he had to obtain his baptismal records from his childhood parish, the Nativity of the Blessed Virgin Mary. Seeing the words "Nativity of the Blessed Virgin Mary" on the certificate, he began to contemplate the mystery of Our Lady's birth. Through the years, his devotion to this mystery grew.

In the summer of 2001, Father Charles DiMascola, a priest friend of Father Noiseux, obtained a small replica of Maria Bambina, made by one of the sisters from the Convent of Maria Bambina in Milan, Italy, to display at his parish of Our Lady of Czestochowa in Turners Falls, Massachusetts. Father Charles obtained the replica through an inquiry to an internet site. Father Donald was surprised to hear of his friend's acquisition, since a friend from his hometown, Elaine Partyka, had tried for years to obtain such an image but had been unable to do so. Elaine is the one who had first introduced Father Donald to the devotion to Maria Bambina. Father Donald immediately called the man who had provided Father Charles with the small replica. The man did not have another small replica; Father Charles had obtained the only image available in that size. A single full-size replica, however, was available. An exquisite copy, it was very expensive.

Fortunately, at this time, he and his sister had just sold a piece of property that they had inherited. Although the obstacle of where to obtain the funds was removed, he still hesitated.

Before he had known of the opportunity to acquire the replica of Maria Bambina, Father Donald had made arrangements to go on pilgrimage to the Shrine of Our Lady of Hope in Pontmain, France. He decided that while he was there, he would ask the Blessed Mother in prayer to help him discern if he should obtain the image. At the shrine, he was amazed to find an image of the Milan Maria Bambina in a side altar of the parish church. Over the years he had visited many famous shrines to Our Lady and dozens of churches in Europe, but this was the first time that he recalled seeing Maria Bambina. He took this as a definite sign that he should not hesitate to purchase the replica for his parish.

Back home, Father Donald hastened to obtain the image. When his friend Father Charles saw it, he suggested that it was so fine that it would attract pilgrims. Father Charles had been an art teacher before entering the seminary, and he suggested that a fitting reliquary be constructed for the beautiful image. He designed the reliquary, and one of his parishioners, Larry Roux, built it, adding his own embellishments to Father Charles's design.

At the same time as preparations were being made for the Maria Bambina to be placed in the church, Father Donald's niece gave birth to twin boys, three months prematurely. For weeks the babies were in precarious health. His sister had the babies' names, Alan and Geoffrey, engraved on small gold hearts, which she placed in the Bambina's crib. The entire family prayed to Maria Bambina that the babies would be healthy. The boys continued to make good progress and continue to do well. The family credits Maria Bambina's intercession in granting this favor.

Father Donald began to feel that he should do something to spread the devotion to Maria Bambina. He asked a parishioner, Marge Craven, to put together a website where people could learn more about the mystery of the nativity of Mary. Devotion to that mystery is a traditional Franciscan devotion, so Marge, who is a third order Franciscan, eagerly set to work to put up the site. She spent months of study and research to get the information shown on the www.mariabambina.org website. Response to the site has been interesting. With no advertising or promotion, the site has received "hits" from all over the world. Inquiries have come from as far as India and Brazil, where people there have expressed a desire to spread this devotion in their countries. Many have remarked that they see the devotion as a call to respect the sanctity of life. When people are first shown a holy card or picture of Maria Bambina, the typical response is enthusiasm and surprise, as if to say, "Why didn't I ever think of Our Lady as a baby before?" Sometimes people are more reserved. Never having heard of the devotion and with there being so many unapproved private revelations, they wonder if Maria Bambina is consistent with the mind of the church. When they are told that the devotion is approved and that Pope St. Pius X and Pope John Paul II have encouraged it, their initial reserve turns to enthusiasm.

Although the pictures of Maria Bambina on the internet are lovely, those who want to visit in person are always welcome at Maria Bambina's beautiful new shrine in Huntington, Massachusetts. The first pilgrimage group came to the shrine in June of 2003.

I recall having been nearly thirty years old when, in looking through a box of family memorabilia, I came across two baby pictures—one of my mother and one of my father. Such pictures were very rare in the days of my parents' childhood, and seeing these pictures for the first time touched me deeply because it called to mind a dimension of their lives that I had never really considered before.

From my earliest childhood, I have been graced with a devotion to Our Blessed Mother. Now, having been a priest for nearly twenty years, I have discovered that just as imag-

ining my own parents as children increased my love for them so, all the more, in contemplating the infancy and childhood of Our Blessed Mother do I come to a deeper love for her. The reflection of Raissa Maritain seems very appropriate in contemplating the image of Maria Bambina. "The Blessed Virgin is the spoiled child of the Blessed Trinity. She knows no law. Everything yields to her in heaven and on earth. The whole of heaven gazes on her with delight. She plays before the ravished eyes of God himself."

—Father Donald Noiseux

Father Noiseux is the pastor of St. Thomas Catholic Church in Huntington, Massachusetts.

For the text of the Garland of the Holy Child Mary, an approved chaplet to promote vocations to the religious life, please visit the special section "Other Faces of Mary" on the author's website: www.annball.com.

The Immaculate Infant Mary (Divina Infantita)
Leon, Mexico

The cult of the Immaculate Infant Mary began with a little-known apparition in Mexico City in 1840 to a Conceptionist sister of the convent of St. Joseph of Grace. On the feast of the Three Kings, while she was in prayful adoration of the Child Jesus in the manger scene, she began to wonder, "Why isn't the Virgin honored in her infancy and celebrated with happy songs like the Child Jesus?" Just as she thought this, she saw a beautiful little girl, dressed like a queen, floating in the air in a reclining position. The vision seemed to say, "I will give those who honor me in my infancy the things they ask me for because this is something the people have forgotten to do."

To read more about the Immaculate Infant Mary, please visit the special section "Other Faces of Mary" on the author's website: www.annball.com.

The Young Mary

The Holy Child Mary
Worldwide

I came to love the child Mary through my devotion to St. Anne, who taught her daughter to read. Teaching has taught me to see my students developmentally: the student I encounter today was formed by a past I only partially comprehend, just as what he will become is a mystery. So in embracing the child Mary, like St. Anne, I embrace the potential for holiness in each of them.

—Susan Kerr

Susan Kerr teaches English to students from around the world in Austin, Texas.

For more information on images of the child Mary throughout the world, please visit the special section "Other Faces of Mary" on the author's website: www.annball.com.

*Mary, Daughter of Anne and Joachim
Detroit, Michigan*

The triptych of Anne, Joachim, and Mary expresses their unwavering trust that the Holy Spirit did indeed overshadow them. Mary is holding the scriptures close to her very pregnant stomach. Joachim and Anne are holding their hands on Mary's stomach, feeling the miracle of the virgin birth. Behind Mary's back, Joachim and Anne hold their hands together in an act of faith that all will end well. Such trust led Mary to surrender herself to God. "I am the servant of the Lord. Let it be unto me as you say" (Luke 1:38).
—Father Robert E. Power, C.S.B.

Father Power was pastor of Ste. Anne de Detroit, Michigan, from 1971 to 1980.

See more images and information about this historic church in the special section "Other Faces of Mary" on the author's website: www.annball.com.

The Baker Woman
Tokyo, Japan

St. Ignatius Church is the largest church in the largest urban area in the world—Tokyo. It is also the largest parish in Japan, with over seven thousand members. The high, white tower of this beautiful, modern-style edifice, topped by a cross, can be seen for miles across the city. The community here is an international one, which is easily noticed by visitors who see that the signs that respectfully ask adults to keep off the grass are in three languages. Masses are said here in Japanese, English, Spanish, Indonesian, Polish, Portuguese, and Vietnamese. The parish bulletin details nearby churches and centers where Masses are offered in Burmese, Chinese, French, German, Kachin, Korean, and Tagalog.

In addition to the main sanctuary, the huge center of worship contains a number of small chapels. The Xavier chapel has a stark interior, with gently bubbling water in a low square fountain at the side, which makes it a perfect place for reflection. Although some of the chapels are quiet, the parish itself is not. Lively and bustling, like the city that surrounds it, the church epitomizes the forward march of Catholicism in Japan.

The main sanctuary is bright, simple, and cheerful. In keeping with the Jesuit practice of using symbolism in their churches, the interior dome is in a lotus pattern, which symbolizes enlightenment. Tall, narrow, stained-glass windows bounce colorful lights through the worship space to reflect fluid rainbows of joyous color around the image of the risen Christ above the altar.

Standing humbly at the back of the sanctuary is a modernistic image of Our Lady, sculpted of a type of rough, pale stone. A Japanese-style arrangement of fresh flowers sits on the floor in front of the image as the sole token of affection for her; she is too new to have called forth the *ex votos* and other pious expressions of devotion so often found near the images of Our Lady in older churches.

The artist Nakono Shigeru has portrayed Mary as a young woman dressed in a simple, modest robe and a veil. One notices at once that she appears to be in the early stage of pregnancy, and her hands are clasped in a prayerful attitude in front of her gently swelling belly. As the viewer approaches, his eye is drawn, as if by a magnet, to the folded hands. It is only then, up close, that one realizes that the humble, pregnant virgin is holding a single perfect head of wheat, as if gently offering it to those who draw close to her.

This modernistic statue of Mary, Mother of God, perfectly epitomizes the compelling allegory of the baker woman, so beautifully translated and set to music by Hubert J. Richards in the late 1960s.* The poem was written by the French Christian poet Marie Noel (d. 1967).

The baker woman in her humble lodge
Received a grain of wheat from God.
For nine whole months the grain she stored.
Behold the handmaid of the Lord!
Make us the bread, Mary, Mary
Make us the bread, we need to be fed.

The baker woman took the road which led
To Bethlehem, the House of Bread.
To knead the bread she labored through the night
And brought it forth about midnight.
Bake us the bread, Mary, Mary
Bake us the bread. We need to be fed.

She baked the bread for thirty years
By the fire of her love, and the salt of her tears
By the warmth of a heart so tender and bright
And the bread was golden brown and white.
Bring us the bread, Mary, Mary,
Bring us the bread, we need to be fed.

After thirty years the bread was done.
It was taken to town by her only son;

* Kevin Mayhew, *Hymns Old and New with Supplement* (1980). Kevin Mayhew Ltd., Buxhall, Stowmarket, Suffolk, 1P14 3BW, U.K. Used by permission, license no. 308060. www.kevinmayhewltd.com.

The soft white bread to be given free
To the hungry people of Galilee.
Give us the bread, Mary, Mary
Give us the bread, we need to be fed.

For thirty coins the bread was sold,
And a thousand teeth so cold, so cold,
Tore it to pieces on a Friday noon
When the sun turned black and red the moon.
Break us the bread, Mary, Mary,
Break us the bread, we need to be fed.

And when she saw the bread so white,
The living bread she made at night,
Devoured as wolves might devour a sheep
The bakerwoman began to weep.
Weep for the bread, Mary, Mary,
Weep for the bread, we need to be fed.

But the baker woman's only son
Appeared to his friends when three days had run
On the road which to Emmaus led,
And they knew him in the breaking of bread.
Lift up your head, Mary, Mary
Lift up your head, for now we've been fed.

The baker woman draws her children to her, children of every race and culture, calling them to a school of the Divine. Among creatures, no one knows Christ better than his mother. She teaches "by obtaining for us in abundance the gifts of the Holy Spirit, even as she offers us the incomparable example of her own 'pilgrimage of faith'" (#17, Rosarium Virginis Mariae).

The somber French poetess Marie Noel wrote this Chant du Pain *(The Song of Bread) during the First World War. In translating it, I added a final verse to bring it into line with more recent theology, which does not separate, as people used to, Christ's death from his resurrection. This theology emphasizes the hope of the Christian message. The metaphorical use of the word "bread" refers, of course, to the person of Christ in general, not to his particular presence in the Eucharist. Holy Communion is not given us by Mary but by God.*

—Hubert Richards

A songwriter and the author of over fifty books, Burt Richards is retired, but he continues writing and lecturing on theology, scripture, and ecumenism. He lives with his wife, Clare, an artist and illustrator, in Norwich, England.

The Virgin of Altagracia
Higuey, Dominican Republic

Fondly called the "Little Sister from Higuey" (Tatica from Higuey), the Virgin of Altagracia is dear to the hearts of the Catholics of the Dominican Republic. The Virgin of Altagracia is the patroness of the island, and her name in Spanish means "Our Lady of High Grace." The city's name—Higuey—means "sun" in the native Taino language. Because of its geographical location, the city is the first place on the island to receive the morning sun.

The image has the distinction of having received a papal crown not once but twice. The Virgin of Altagracia was crowned in 1922 during the reign of Pius XI and again in 1979, when Pope John Paul II visited Santo Domingo. The pope personally crowned her with a beautiful tiara of gold and silver and named her the "First Evangelizer of the Americas."

The image is a portrait of the Virgin at the nativity. It is small, about thirteen by eighteen inches, and is painted on cloth. The picture was painted about the turn of the fourteenth century by an unknown artist of the Spanish school. It is framed in an ornate frame of gold, enamel, and precious stones. The frame was crafted by an unknown eighteenth-century artisan, who most likely used the jewelry presented as *ex votos* to the image for his materials. His work is considered one of the finest examples of Dominican gold work.

Through the centuries, the smoke from countless candles and constant handling by clients damaged the picture. Artisans in Spain restored it in 1978, and today it glows with its original color and beauty. The Virgin is shown wearing a blue cloak, a red tunic, and a white scapular, the colors of the Dominican flag. Her devotees see this as symbolic of an anticipation of the country's national identity.

Two of the first European settlers to Hispanola (today's Dominican Republic), Alfonso and Antonio Trejo, brought the portrait to the island some time before 1502 and eventually donated it to the parish church at Higuey. Historical documents show that the Virgin was honored under the title Altagracia as early as 1502 and that the painting was brought to the island within the first years of its discovery by the Trejo brothers.

The first shrine was finished in 1572. The cornerstone for a magnificent modern cathedral was set in 1954. The painting was translated to the new shrine, now a minor basilica, in 1971. Annually, on January 21, thousands of visitors flock to the basilica to celebrate the Dominican victory over the French in the 1691 Battle of Sabana. Also known as the Battle of Limonada, the Dominicans had appealed to the Virgin for help and saw their victory as a grace given through her intercession.

The new basilica, designed by French architects A. Dunoyer de Segonzac and Pierre Dupre, was inaugurated in 1971. It has a unique, avant-garde construction and is an outstanding modern architectural work. Its concrete structure is dominated by a high arch. In order to highlight the architecture, a new system of lighting was installed in 2002 which bathes the concrete exterior in dramatic color from sunset to midnight.

Just as with many other images of Our Lady, the Virgin of Altagracia has a pious tradition connected with its origin. The province of the Dominican Republic known as La Altagracia is a cattle-raising region, because of its extensive plains. Higuey is now the main city of the area. As tradition has it, many years ago, one of the original Spanish colonists, a wealthy and esteemed rancher, lived with his family in the region of Duey. It was his custom to take his cattle to the city of Ozam for sale. On each trip, he carried home presents for his two young daughters. Early one January, as he was preparing for the trip, his oldest daughter asked him to bring her some of the things that all girls delight in: laces, ribbons, a new dress, and other ornaments. The youngest daughter, barely fourteen years old, was deeply religious. She begged her father to bring her an image of the Virgin of the Highest Grace, telling him that she had seen it in a dream. He had never heard of such a name for the Holy Virgin, but she assured him that he would find it on his trip.

After selling his cattle in the city, the good father easily found and purchased the gifts for his oldest daughter. Although he searched throughout the city, asking the councilors and even the archbishop, he could not find an image known as the Virgin of Altagracia. Everyone he asked told him that such an image did not exist.

On his return, he stopped to spend the night at the home of an old friend near Los Dos Rios. At supper, the loving father sadly told his hosts about his failure to find the gift of the Virgin's picture for his daughter. An old man with a white beard, a stranger who had stopped at the house asking for shelter, was seated in the room. On hearing the rancher's words, he stood up and approached the table where the family was seated. "What do you mean the Virgin of Altagracia doesn't exist?" he said. "I have brought her with me!" Then, reaching into his saddlebag, the stranger pulled out a roll of cloth, which he unfolded to display a beautiful image of Mary.

The precious image showed the Virgin, beautiful and serene, worshiping her newborn babe asleep on a bed of hay. Behind her shoulder, the humble St. Joseph was watching the mother and child, with his hand sheltering the flame of a candle, just as he sheltered the Holy Family. The Virgin wore a blue cloak sprinkled with stars, and over her left shoulder the star of Bethlehem shone brightly.

The rancher was overjoyed to recognize in the picture the image of the Virgin Mary at the moment of her highest grace—the divine motherhood of Christ. Happily, he and his friends invited the traveler to spend the night. The rancher planned to offer the man a generous sum to purchase the picture as a gift for his daughter. The following morning, they were surprised to find that the mysterious stranger had disappeared, leaving the picture.

The father, carrying the beautiful image with him, returned home full of joy. According to tradition, his youngest daughter, accompanied by several other pious persons, met him near an orange tree, where he gave her his precious gift. Even today, an orange tree is kept growing near the basilica to mark the spot where the veneration of the cult of the Virgin of Altagracia began.

The Virgin's feast day, January 6, is celebrated by Masses, all-night vigils, singing, dancing, and festivals.

For me, no matter how she is portrayed, the Virgin Mary represents much by the fact that she is the Mother of Jesus, the Son of God. The words of Christ from the cross, "Mother, there is your son; son there is your Mother," have always echoed in my mind, and in many moments of uncertainty and suffering I pray to Mary for consolation. From her example, we receive the greatest of lessons: humility, selflessness, unconditional love, conviction, and resignation.

For many, the choice of the Virgin of Altagracia to represent the Dominican Republic represents a place of healing, such as at the great shrines of Lourdes and Fatima. For others, the God of the Old Testament is an awesome God. Even in his great benevolence he often inspires fear. In his humanity, Jesus makes God more accessible to his people, especially through Mary. It is with Mary and through Mary that the illiterate, the less cultured, the poor and the humble can find a respected intermediary to speak to that powerful God who can forgive all our sins. These people, especially, seem to feel that Mary can do a good job of "getting God's ear."

—Carlos Cabral

Carlos Cabral, originally from the Dominican Republic, is a businessman in Miami, Florida.

Notre Dame du Guiaudet
St. Nicolas du Pelem, Brittany, France

Along the picturesque north coast of Brittany, there are a number of unique and interesting images of the Virgin Mary at childbirth. They are known as *gesine* images. The word comes from Old French and means "lying down." Locally, they are called *Vierges couchées,* and they date from the late sixteenth or early seventeenth centuries. One of these is known as Notre Dame du Guiaudet.

The image of Notre Dame du Guiaudet is in the parish of Corlay-St. Nicolas of Pelem. At Lanrivain, there is a chapel and pilgrimage site dedicated to this "lying Virgin," who is reclining on a couch with her Divine Son near her. The image of the Virgin, wearing a beautiful blue and gold gown, lies in a recess behind the altar.

The devotion to Notre Dame du Guiaudet began in the last years of the reign of King Louis XIV, during a famine in 1692. It has been dear to the hearts of Breton Catholics for over three hundred years, although the chapel was closed during the dark days of the French Revolution.

Near the end of the seventeenth century, there was a small village with a few thatched cottages in what was then known as Coatcoustronnec (now called Lanrivain). There had once been a chapel there, but, long ago, it fell into ruin and disappeared. Archaeologists have found evidence of a farming settlement in the area from the fifth and sixth centuries, possibly begun by Britons from the West Country. Tradition holds that the area was Christianized in the year 71 by Drennalus, a disciple of Joseph of Arimathia and Nicodemus. In 1692, the cult to the Mother of God was revived here through messages given to a poor peasant named Yves-Claude Allain.

The son of pious and humble workers, Claude was born in a nearby village around the year 1658. Following their example, he was a good, hard-working, young man. He married and moved to Coatcoustronnec, where he became known as an excellent husband and father and a devout Catholic. Claude set up a small chapel in his home, where he taught his twelve children a living faith and a deep devotion to the Virgin Mary.

One day in 1692, the family breadbasket was empty, and there was only a small bowl of flour in the pantry. Taking his rosary in hand, Claude began walking toward a nearby village, hoping to purchase a little more flour with the few coins he had left.

As the last strains of the *Angelus* flowed from the bell tower and the sun was rising over the fields and flowers, even the birds seemed to join in the heavenly concert. But poor Claude could not see the morning charms. His heart was heavy as he prayed his beads, begging the Virgin to aid him in feeding his family. As he crossed over a little stream near the fountain of Our Lady, he heard a voice of incomparable sweetness. He was surprised to see in front of him a beautiful woman whom he instantly believed was the Mother from Heaven. She spoke to Claude in his native language, telling him to go to the priest at Bothoa and inform him that the Virgin wished a chapel built in this place in her honor and in honor of St. John, the beloved disciple. She told him that as proof that she was truly the Virgin Mary, he would witness a miracle that very day: the small amount of flour that he had at home would be enough to feed his family for many days.

The woman disappeared, and at first Claude was struck dumb, seized with an instinctive fear. Soon, however, his soul recovered its normal calm. He stood motionless at the site of the apparition for some time, then rushed home to report the encounter to his wife and children.

On hearing his report, Claude's wife did not hesitate and began at once to knead the small amount of flour. The flour began to grow just like the handful of flour in the jar of the widow of Zarephath in the time of the prophet Elijah (1 Kings 17:8-16).

On seeing this, Claude left quickly to find the priest, as the Virgin had directed. He ran rapidly to the house where the priest lived and excitedly reported the exact words told to him in the apparition. The rector, Gregoire Raul, a pious and humble priest, had been pastor for eleven years. Because of some earlier problems, he had become prudent and a bit distrustful. Although he knew Claude as his best parishioner, the priest reacted with incredulity, telling Claude that he was exaggerating and forbidding him to speak of the apparition again.

Claude sadly returned home, wondering if he had been dreaming. On his arrival, however, the children showed him the fresh baked breads his wife had just taken from the oven. So he began praying to the Mother of God, asking her how to convince the priest of her wishes. The Virgin appeared to him again and urged him to return to the rector and repeat her request. Claude's second visit produced no better results than the first, and he returned home heavy-hearted at failing in his mission.

The priest, meanwhile, remembered that Claude normally had good sense and decided to make a little inquiry about the alleged miracle. He interviewed Claude's wife and children separately, and the entire family confirmed the prodigy.

Mary appeared to Claude a third time, telling him to return to the priest yet again and to have confidence that this time his words would be believed. On this occasion, the priest welcomed Claude and begged pardon for his previous lack of faith.

The news of the apparitions soon spread, and some town folk went to see the place where the Virgin wished her chapel built. At the site, a small wooden sculpture of the Virgin holding her Child was found. Although the people accepted this as a further miracle, the discovery may simply confirm the tradition of a previous chapel at the site.

Father Gregoire organized a procession of expiation, promised to build the requested chapel, and, with trembling hands, he set the image of Mary on a rock and piously venerated it. The people immediately constructed a rustic shelter to serve until a proper chapel could be built.

The Virgin began to shower her graces over the pilgrims who came to venerate her image. Gifts poured in for the construction of the requested chapel. By the end of 1693, a new chapel had been built with six transepts and an apse. In 1901, the sanctuary was enriched with stained-glass windows. A bell tower constructed in 1920 holds a carillon of six bells, which ring popular canticles and which were electrified in 1964. The place of the apparition was covered, and a fountain was constructed there.

During the French Revolution, pilgrimages to Guiaudet were interrupted; and at one time, in 1794, vandals broke into the chapel and pulled down the statue. In spite of their fear, faithful Catholics came and replaced the Virgin in her niche. At night, the townspeople would come in secret to recite the rosary before the closed door of the church. After the Revolution, the cult of Notre Dame du Guiaudet recovered its ancient vigor, and pilgrimages began again.

The great pardon held on the first Sunday of May is always a beautiful manifestation of Marian Breton piety. An expression of popular religiosity, from the fifteenth century, pilgrims would gather in large numbers to ask for pardons and indulgences. These assemblies, which the clergy called pardons, are colorful displays, with participants carrying banners and wearing traditional costumes. The pilgrims recite the rosary, venerate the miraculous statue of the Virgin, drink from the fountain, confess, and receive communion. Although no official declaration has ever been made with regard to the supernatural character of the apparitions, Pope

St. Pius X enriched the great pardon of Notre Dame du Guiaudet with an indulgence. A second pardon is held here on the first Sunday in August.

Le Yaudet (Ploulec'h, Côtes-d'Armor) granite promontory, overlooking the estuary of the Lannion river in northwestern Brittany, has been constantly occupied from early prehistory to the present day. In the Late Iron Age (second to first century BC), the headland was defended by massive earthworks, still visible today, civilian occupation continuing into the Early Roman period. At the end of the third century AD, because of widespread trouble in the western provinces of the Roman Empire, the promontory was refortified and garrisoned. As our recent excavation program has shown, this presence was sustained throughout the whole of the very Early Middle Ages (fifth to seventh century AD), at a time when colonists, coming from southwestern Britain, settled in the Armorican peninsula.

The creation of a monastery at Le Yaudet, in the early decades of the sixth century AD, has been ascertained in the 2002 season of excavations. Its remains, however, are so scanty that there is no telling whether the early church was built on the terrace where the nineteenth-century church now stands. This is indeed quite likely, as the present church, rebuilt in the 1860s, includes earlier elements, some of which may date back to the Romanesque period. The baroque reredos, including the famous Lying Virgin, certainly belongs to the sixteenth-century rebuilding phase, when the age-old structure was beautified to serve a major local pilgrimage. The touchingly naive wooden image of the Virgin lying in bed with the young Jesus, fashioned after other contemporary depictions of Our Lady, was later imitated in a number of Breton churches, including those of Lanrivain and Kergrist.

—Patrick Galliou

Patrick Galliou is currently professor in the Université de Bretagne Occidentale, Brest, France. He has excavated a number of Late Iron Age and Roman sites in western Brittany, including Le Yaudet (with Barry Cunliffe, professor of European Archaeology, University of Oxford). His published works include *The Bretons* (with Michael Jones) (Oxford: Blackwell, 1991). He is a Fellow of the Society of Antiquaries of London.

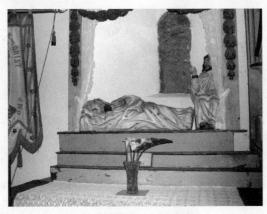

Reclining Virgin, Chapel of Kergrist,
Brittany, France

Mary Most Pure

Our Lady of Chapi
Arequipa, Peru

Thousands of pilgrims annually cross the desert from the city of Arequipa, wending their way through a narrow, barren valley to a shining white shrine in the Andean region of Peru. Here, Our Lady of Chapi waits to greet her pious devotees. The Virgin of Chapi is of a type known as a *candelaria,* an image of purity symbolized by the candle she holds in her right hand.

The *candelaria* devotion, sometimes called the "Purisma," was very popular among the early Spanish missionaries working in the Southern Andes. A number of other images of this type are popular in this region, including the Virgin of Cocharcas in Peru and the Virgin of Copacabana in Bolivia.

The Virgin of Chapi is of Spanish origin, and the image is approximately two feet tall. In her right hand she holds a candle and a small basket containing two doves. She cradles her Divine Son on her left arm and holds a rosary in her left hand. In keeping with Hispanic tradition, the image is dressed in richly embroidered clothing. Inside the temple, both she and the babe wear beautiful crowns, and Our Lady wears a regal cloak and sometimes a decorative sash. When the Virgin of Chapi goes out to meet her clients in procession, however, her hair is braided and falls in graceful plaits similar to those of the women of the region. She and her son don a protective cloak, and each wears a large Peruvian hat. The large, dark eyes of the Virgin of Chapi are compelling. They seem to invite the repentant pilgrim to the love and mercy of her Son.

In the eighteenth century, pilgrimages were held in conjunction with the feast of the Candelaria, just before Lent began. In the nineteenth century, the feast was officially changed to May 1 because the early spring weather was often bad. By 1907, a second day for celebration was added and set for September 8, the feast of the Nativity of Mary. During the last century, this date has become the most popular, and thousands of inhabitants of Arequipa, the largest city in southern Peru, leave their homes and walk all night in freezing temperatures for sixty miles, many of them carrying heavy stones as a sign of penance, to reach the shrine on September 8.

Chapi's fervent devotees walk about fifteen hours to reach the shrine, which is eight thousand feet above sea level. Because of the high altitude, many of them lean on rustic walking sticks. As they reach their first stop, Tres Cruces, they leave some of the stones, called *apachetas,* symbolically beginning to shed their weariness and sins. They stop again at Alto de Hornilla and then at Siete Toldos, leaving more *apachetas,* which are lit by the countless candles they are carrying.

When the pilgrims reach the sparkling shrine made of sillar, a form of volcanic rock, the Virgin of Chapi comes out to greet them, borne aloft in a joyful procession over a carpet of flower petals. Before attending one of the many Masses, pilgrims pile their final penance rocks outside the shrine. After the Mass, they go to the image of Our Lady and cover themselves with her cape as a sign of seeking her protection. Some drink water from the nearby fountain. That night, all are in a festive mood. Fireworks light the evening sky, and vendors hawk all manner of food from booths next to the sanctuary. At last, the weary pilgrims board the many busses for the trip back to Arequipa.

The devotion to the Virgin of Chapi is the most popular Marian devotion in southern Peru. It contains traditional elements common to other Marian devotions: an image suddenly discovered, a fountain appearing miraculously, and clear signs of where the Virgin indicates she wishes a place of worship to be built.

According to tradition, the image of the Virgin of Chapi was found at the foot of a mountain in the late sixteenth century by a group of pilgrims traveling by horseback from the city of Moquegua to Arequipa. The image was taken to the town of Churajon, but in 1600 the area was swept by the eruption of the Huayana Putina volcano, and the surviving villagers were forced to relocate.

They brought their beloved image of the Virgin with them to a valley called Cheipi, which the Spaniards, finding it hard to pronounce, rechristened with the simpler name of Chapi.

The original small chapel was located along the road connecting Arequipa and Moquegua, the two most important Spanish cities in the region. The devotion soon became popular among travelers. In 1760, precious metals were discovered in the area, and an influx of miners arrived, who also became devout clients of the Virgin of Chapi.

A letter written in 1743 by Bishop Manuel Chavez de la Rosa makes reference to the popularity of the image of Chapi, "which attracts a significant crowd of pilgrims for the feast of the Candelaria." By 1798, the inhabitants of the region complained to the Pastor of Pocsi, Father Juan De Dios Jose Tamayo, about the "disorder and chaos" brought to the town by the pilgrims; so the priest ordered the image to be moved to the town of Sogay.

A procession was formed to move the image to her new place, but as they neared the town of Chapi, they were suddenly hit with a paralyzing sandstorm. Each time the group tried to continue their trip to Sogay, another phenomenon took place: first an earthquake, then another storm. Finally, they realized the image wished to remain where it was. Father Tamayo ordered a shrine built on the spot. Here the Virgin greeted her devoted clients for seventy years.

On August 13, 1868, a violent earthquake completely destroyed the shrine. As workers dug through the rubble, they were amazed to find the image intact. The news spread quickly, bringing even more pilgrims to the temporary temple built out of wood. In February 1893, construction began on a completely new shrine, to be made of sillar; but the lack of water in the area made the construction slow and painful. At last, a group of masons had had enough and decided to leave the project. One of the masons called on the Virgin for help, and suddenly he felt he was being guided to a nearby spot. Here he found a fountain of crystal-clear water. Today, this fountain remains one of the key spots visited by the pilgrims to Chapi. The shrine was completed and dedicated in 1907.

On June 23, 2000, an earthquake again shocked the southern Peruvian region, bringing significant destruction to Arequipa and Moquehua, and damaging the shrine of Our Lady of Chapi so badly that the Virgin had to be translated to the Yanahuara district in the city of Arequipa. She is there now, thus bringing to a halt the tradition of the pilgrimage. The reconstruction of her shrine, considering the cost and the poverty of the region, will take several years, maybe decades.

I was at the sanctuary of the Virgin of Chapi from March 1999 until January 2002. There I was stationed with the community of priests of the Institute of the Incarnate Word, who are dedicated to the contemplative life and who serve the pilgrims at the shrine. For me, the experience there was a way to live concretely my perpetual vow of slavery to Mary, which I had made October 12, 1992, in San Rafael, Argentina. Like the little Indian Juan Diego, who lived his life in the service of the Virgin of Guadalupe in Mexico, and the black man Manuel, who was consecrated to and cared for the Virgin of Lujan in Argentina, so also I could experience the immense joy of serving Our Lady of Chapi for three years as her unworthy servant. Of course, in my case, I had neither the humility nor the virtues that adorned these two faithful servants of the Virgin. Seeing the miracles of conversion that arose in the hearts of the pilgrims only by looking at the most beautiful eyes of the Virgin, I learned to understand more fully the immense love that the Mother of God has for sinners. Seeing the tender and sweet love that the Peruvian people have for the Virgin of Chapi, I learned that my own devotion should be more tender.

—P. José Antonio Marcone, I.V.E.

Father Marcone is a priest of the Institute of the Incarnate Word now stationed in La Pintaus, Chile.

The Virgin of Loreto of La Bahia
Goliad, Texas

Presidio La Bahia is the oldest fort in the western United States and one of few surviving examples of a Spanish Colonial mission/presidio complex in North America. Designated a National Historic Landmark in 1967, the presidio is owned and operated by the Catholic Diocese of Victoria. The chapel was originally erected to serve the soldiers stationed at the fort, their families, and the other citizens of La Bahia. Although the presidio is now a historic site open to the public, its chapel still operates as a community church, serving the spiritual needs of the area's Catholics—Spanish, Mexican, Texan, and American in turn—since 1779. Mass is celebrated weekly on Sunday evening.

In the early 1700s, the Spanish government decided to occupy the Texas coast in order to keep foreigners, especially the French, out of the area. The area was called Texas because when the first DeLeon-Massanet expedition entered, the native Americans living there greeted the Spaniards with the words "Techas! Techas!" which means "friends" The Spaniards applied the name to the tribe, from which it evolved into the name for the entire state. The Franciscan missionaries had long begged to begin a mission for the coastal Indians; so it was decided to establish a mission and a presidio. In the years 1719 to 1722, the Marquis de Aguayo led an expedition into Texas from Mexico. The last of the Spanish expeditions to enter Texas, it was also one of the most important, because it secured Spain's hold on the territory for over a hundred years.

Three Franciscan priests from the college of Zacatecas accompanied Aguayo: Father Augustine Patron y Guzman, Father Matias Saenz, and Father Antonio Margil. They planned to work among the Karankawa Indians of the Cocos, Cujames, and Copanes tribes. All three were remarkable men; both Patron and Margil had a reputation for great holiness, even in their lifetime. Fathers Diego Zapata and Ignacio Bahena soon came to join them at Mission Espíritu Santo. Father Juan Antonio Pena was the official chaplain and chronicler of the expedition, and his diary of the trip is invaluable to contemporary historians.

The Marquis of San Miguel de Aguayo (Joseph Virto de Vera) was a wealthy and highly esteemed rancher living in Coahuila when he was appointed to lead the expedition. He gathered men and supplies, and took with him nearly five hundred men, about five thousand horses and mules, and large herds of cattle and sheep. The expedition took possession of La Bahia del Espíritu Santo in the name of his majesty the king and raised the cross and royal standard on April 4, 1721. The presidio was given the official name of Nuestra Señora de Loreto La Bahia del Espíritu Santo.

Aguayo had a strong devotion to Mary. In his diary, Father Pena wrote that in addition to his zeal for the king,

> With the greatest complacency he has shown his love for sowing the Gospel Truth among so many souls who live in the sad shadows of mankind. [The Marquis] also displayed his intention of returning the Province to its rightful ruler. It is also known that Our Lord the King [may God protect him] has a Catholic, Christian zeal to extend his dominion over the entire world and thus bring Christ,

the Sun of Justice, for all to see. Our guiding light in this enterprise has been Our Lady of Pilar whom the Governor selected as guide and patroness. As a shield on the Texas frontier he left this Tower of David so that she might protect it just as she had done when the Most Holy Virgin left her image and column of Non Plus Ultra at Zaragoza which was then the edge of the known world of the Spanish people. The Plus Ultra has likewise been placed [on this frontier] to protect the most remote people who have been discovered in America by the Spaniards. In an act of thanksgiving His Lordship concluded the expedition yesterday with a beautiful and solemn fiesta in honor of Our Lady. We implored not only the maintenance of that Province, but also for the addition of all [other Provinces] where the sun might shine to the Crown and dominion of our Catholic Phillip, for in this manner they will come into the Kingdom of God which is praised by all creatures for all eternity.

The chapel was named after a famous shrine of the same name in Italy, and also because its location was among the laurels (Texas sweet bay), which grew profusely along the Texas Gulf Coast. The word Loreto is derived from the word "laurel." In addition to the supplies and men required for the new establishment, the devout marquis brought with him a beautiful little wooden image of Our Lady of Loreto and enshrined her in the chapel of the presidio.

Problems soon arose between the Indians and the soldiers, whose leader was not fitted for the job; and the Franciscans advised moving the mission to a more favorable spot about ten miles inland. Both mission and presidio were moved by 1726, and the padres began working among the Aranama Indians living there. The little image of Our Lady was taken to her new home. Here, in the area known as Mission Valley, the mission remained and prospered for the next twenty-six years. Many Indians were baptized and became good Christians.

In spite of the favorable location and prosperity, Don Jose Escandon, who had been authorized by the crown to rearrange the location of the presidios in Texas, recommended that the presidio and mission be moved to an area on the lower San Antonio River because it was a better location for a fort to guard the main road from Mexico to San Antonio and east Texas. The move was made about 1749. As before, Our Lady accompanied her Spanish children to the new location near today's city of Goliad.

In the twilight years of the mission, the little image had become dirty and defaced. It was rescued by one of the priests, Father White, and taken to San Antonio to be restored before being returned to La Bahia.

In the early nineteenth century, political turbulence began which culminated in the Texas war for independence. La Bahia and its chapel were taken from the Catholics and went through several owners.

The years after the Texas revolution were not good to Presidio La Bahia. The walls and buildings (except for the chapel) within the presidio decayed and slowly collapsed. The chapel was used as a residence in the late 1840s and early 1850s. This use was frowned on by the local Catholics, who wanted the chapel returned to the church.

An act of the Republic of Texas in 1841 returned much former church property, but in 1844 Presidio La Bahia and its Our Lady of Loreto Chapel were given to the town of Goliad as part of a four league grant of land. The town of Goliad would not return the chapel to the Catholic Church. In 1853, the Catholic Church purchased the chapel from the town of Goliad for $1,000. When the Catholic Church received the title in 1855, it included "the entire old fort." The chapel has been used as a place of worship since then, but the fort was in ruins until restored.

During the mid-1960s, the Kathryn Stoner O'Connor Foundation funded a restoration project, and the fort was rebuilt to its 1836 appearance. Presidio La Bahia was designated a National Historic Landmark.

In keeping with her Spanish heritage, the little Virgin of

Loreto at La Bahia is dressed by the women of the parish. Single women customarily sew new clothes for her from the scraps of their prettiest dress. They smile when they say they hope that the Virgin will be grateful and send them a good man in return for the favor.

The feast of Our Lady of Loreto is celebrated at the presidio with a special Mass and ceremony.

Our Lady of Loreto lights our journey of faith and shows us how to let go and trust. She is the best example we have to believe in God's will as she did. She gives us the strength and courage for what is sent to us. My devotion to her was a decisive turning point in my life. The turning point has been my inner journey of devotion to Our Lady. She shows me the way to her son and Father. Every rosary bead enables me to find confidence in her without reserve. I now know I can sample her mercy by opening my heart. Her influence has strengthened my spiritual life and shown me how to obtain peace from within. I try to visit her often because it reminds me of the comfort and understanding she always offers when we deliver ourselves to her spirit and grace.

—Michelle Rubio

Ms. Rubio is a graduate of Southwest Texas State University, a businesswoman. She is active in the community of historic Goliad, Texas.

Our Lady of Nyaunglebin
Myanmar

From the time in 1855 when Our Lady appeared to the French peasant girl Bernadette at the grotto of Massabielle, copies of the Lourdes image of the Immaculate Conception have spread throughout the world. In countries far from the site of her apparitions, strong devotion has grown up in many places, with veneration of the copies of the image and showers of graces. In each place, local customs surround the celebration of this universal image of Mary.

One copy of the Lourdes image in the Union of Myanmar is known as Our Lady of Nyaunglebin. Here, in spite of persecution by the government, her devoted Burmese people remain faithful to the Queen of Heaven.

Catholicism entered the country now officially called Myanmar in the seventeenth century, when missionaries were sent by the Propaganda Fide in Rome from Cochin, China, and from Tonking to Siam. Since then, the borders and the name of the country have changed a number of times. Siam, Mandalay, Rangoon, and Burma are all names that were familiar to the world before the country was renamed the Union of Myanmar in 1988. Today, Catholics form a small but dedicated minority of only about one and one-half percent of the population. Burmese Catholics cling to their faith in spite of persecution by the military junta that has governed the country since 1962. In 2003, Father Vito del Prete, secretary of the Pontifical Missionary Union, inaugurated a meeting in Rome on the "Freedom of Religion and Human Rights Denied in Burma." He said that the church there has not given up its "evangelizing mission," which is stronger in that Southeast Asian nation because it is "close to the poor, those who suffer, and the oppressed." He continued by reporting that "Missions cannot have schools, Christians are prohibited any external manifestation, [and] any kind of apostolate or meeting, and communities are regarded as accomplices of the northern guerrillas."

Once, Burma was a major oil and mineral producer and the world's largest exporter of rice. Wealthy and envied by Southeast

Asian neighbors, the people took pride in their free educational system. Today, the country is poor and is one of the world's major refugee-producing countries. Many people have fled their homes and villages to escape forced labor and other abuses of human rights. Burmese immigration to the United States began in the early 1950s. Many of the immigrants settled in California. There, a small but active group of Catholics treasure their memories of their home country and their devotion to Our Lady.

The national Marian pilgrimage center of Myanmar is in the town called Nyaunglebin, about one hundred miles from Yangon (Rangoon). Here the Lourdes image is known as Our Lady of Nyaunglebin. Her feast day is celebrated for three days in February, and many Catholics, and even non-Catholics who have heard of her, go there by car, plane, train, or bullock carts. In spite of the government restrictions, thousands dare to attend the annual festival. During the joyful celebration, there is a candlelight procession every evening when the image is carried from the church around the town.

A Burmese American Catholic from California recalls attending the festival in the 1970s along with her husband and her sister. The image of Our Lady of Nyaunglebin was dressed in a beautiful blue-sequined mantle and crown and was lavishly decorated with flowers. A wooden stand held between two long bamboo poles was also covered with flowers and was used to carry the image in the procession. The entire celebration had a joyous, yet respectful, atmosphere.

In 1892, Bishop Begandek sent Father Perroy to Pegu Division to begin missionary work there. He began a mission around the villages of Nyaunglebin. That August, Mr. Pu Lu, sixty years of age, and his wife became the first in the area to receive the sacrament of Baptism. Later that year, the bishop assigned Father Mignot to the mission. This priest stayed at the railway workers' guest house and built the small two-story church, which still stands. Here the image of Our Lady was first installed in Burma.

In 1900, a beautiful shrine was built near the church, and on

April 30, 1902, the first feast of Our Lady of Lourdes/Nyaung-Lay-Bin was celebrated. In 1917, a grotto was added and an additional statue was donated anonymously.

Our Lady's reign in Burma has not been without troubles. In 1928, a mentally disturbed man pulled the statue down from its base in the grotto and wrecked it. Father Mignot was able to replace the statue with another from France. Father Mignot died in 1937 and was buried in the church. During World War II, the church was destroyed by Japanese bombs, and the tomb of Father Mignot was plundered and damaged. A priest from a nearby parish collected the remains and buried them in the Catholic cemetery. In 1977, Father Peter U Thet Lwin, the parish priest, transferred the remains to their present location at the back of Our Lady's grotto.

At one time, Japanese soldiers had their base in the church compound. They broke the statue of Our Lady and threw it into the pond. After the war, the image was rescued and repaired. Because of the occupation during the war, Our Lady's feast could not be celebrated in Nyaunglebin, although it was observed in several neighboring villages each year until 1956. In 1957 Father Lucas Wee started celebrating the annual feast at Our Lady's shrine and in the town of Nyaunglebin. Nyaunglebin is designated as the National Marian Pilgrimage for all Catholic dioceses in the country.

The 102nd anniversary of the annual National Marian Pilgrimage (feast of Our Lady of Lourdes) at Nyaunglebin was held in 2004. One Burmese American couple who attended reported that one of the most beautiful parts of the three-day celebration was the evening procession by candlelight. Pilgrims sing and pray the rosary along the three-mile route around the city. The image of the Virgin leads the procession. The statue is decorated with a long veil and roses. Long wreaths of jasmine are hung from her hand. A girl dressed in white holds a big silver bowl, which is used for collecting donations along the way. Eventually, the procession returns to the church compound, where a huge platform is ready for an open-air Benediction service.

From the secular viewpoint, the area has not changed much since the 1970s. The roads are dusty, muddy, and filled with holes; but spiritually, we see that many come, trusting in God, and their faith is very strong. And all the dioceses of the whole of Myanmar are present.

Today, Our Lady of Nyaunglebin stands in solidarity with her suffering Burmese children. For them, as for us all, she is a symbol of hope.

This is a national pilgrimage for all Catholics, but on our pilgrimage, we see that many Buddhists attend it, even a few from other religions, such as Hindus, Muslims, etc. They also joined in giving donations. We are grateful to God for touching the hearts of the Governing Board to allow this annual National Marian Pilgrimage to take place each year and with such humongous celebrations affecting the whole town of Nyaunglebin. Our Lord, through His Mother, Our Lady, touches the hearts of all the people there, those who attend it and those who observe and see or hear it (as the audio speakers are indeed very loud). The procession is around the whole town. As a matter of fact, we saw that about eighty percent of the food stalls at the pilgrimage were sponsored by Buddhists, Muslims, and other religions.

—a Burmese American who attended
the 2004 celebrations in Myanmar

Mary, Our Mother

Our Lady of the Garden
Genoa, Italy

Venerable John Henry Cardinal Newman (1801–90) defined the mystical meaning of garden as "a place of spiritual repose, stillness, peace, refreshment and delight." Throughout history, the "garden" has been used allegorically to express the ultimate in perfection. The home of our first parents was a garden; Christ on the cross promises to take the good thief to paradise, a garden of pleasure. In the Song of Songs the writer speaks of his bride as "a garden enclosed." For centuries this title has been accommodated to the Blessed Virgin, and the title Our Lady of the Garden is one that is used in the Litany of Mary.

The ancient painting known as *Our Lady of the Garden* does not itself depict a garden. Rather, it received its name from the location where the image was originally placed at the end of the fifteenth century. In the spring of 1493, the city of Genoa was suffering from a serious cholera epidemic. The city has always been known for its seafarers, so the nearby coastal towns were also in danger. A pious woman, Maria dei Quercio, known as "Turchina," vowed to make a public expression of gratitude if her family was spared from the sickness. When they remained free of cholera, she commissioned the painter Benedict Borzone to paint a picture of the Virgin. The painting also depicted Sts. Rocco and Sebastian, popular Renaissance patrons against plagues and diseases.

Feeling that more people would see the painting if it were put in a public place rather than inside a church, Turchina directed the artist to paint it on the wall that extended from the Palace of the Captain (mayor of the town) to the sea. The painting expresses vividly the power and goodness of Mary. The Virgin holds the Infant Jesus with her left hand, and with her right she holds up his tiny arm to bless the city and all who pass by. The words of the angelic salutation, *"Ave gratia plena"* (Hail, full of grace) circle the Virgin's head; above the figures we read the biblical phrase from the Song of Songs: *"Hortus conclusus"* (enclosed garden).

Although paintings showing the Virgin holding up the Christ Child's arm in blessing were common at this time, they always depicted the blessing being given to the child John the Baptist. Here the little king's blessing extends to all. Soon known as the *"Madonna dell' Orto"* (Madonna of the Garden), the image immediately began to attract devotion. The devotion increased dramatically thirty years later when another epidemic swept the area, and the first altar was built at the little shrine so that Mass could be said there.

Through the years, devotion to Our Lady increased.

Although constantly exposed to the weather and the salty sea air, the painting, almost miraculously, remained fresh and undamaged.

Nearly a century later, in 1609, devotion had waned. The time of great need in the midst of pestilence had passed, and people slowly began to forget Our Lady's aid, simply passing by the little shrine without stopping.

One morning a devout midwife, Geronima Turrio, stopped on her way to assist a woman of Chiavari. As she contemplated the still beautiful face of the Virgin in the painting, she was overwhelmed with sadness because of the abandonment of devotion there. On the night of December 17th of that year, Geronima was awakened by a bright light in her room. In the center of the light she saw a beautiful woman dressed in clothing that resembled the garments worn by the Virgin in the painting of the *Madonna dell'Orto.* Geronima woke up her neighbors to tell them about the vision, and at the first light hurried to the shrine to test her memory and see if the painting was indeed of the same woman she had seen. With joy, she realized the two were identical, and with great love and devotion she begged the Madonna to see to the safety of her son, a sailor at sea.

Returning home, Geronima received word that her son was grievously ill, so she immediately retraced her steps to the little shrine to beg her heavenly protectress for aid. Within ten days, her son, Bartholomew, returned home completely cured. Our Lady's fervent devotee returned time and again to decorate the little shrine with candles and flowers. Others joined her, and soon the nearly abandoned little shrine became a place rich in graces and piety. Favors and acts of piety multiplied.

A year later, July 2, 1610, there was a second apparition of Our Lady of the Garden. A deeply religious young man, Sebastiano Descalzo, was praying as he walked along the road near the garden wall. Suddenly, he saw the figure of a woman moving slowly toward the square in the bright light of two torches apparently held by invisible spirits. At first frightened, he began to run toward the sea, away from the vision; but as he reached the nearby church of St. Roch, his curiosity overcame him and he turned to see where the lady was going. It seemed to float to the front of the little shrine, which became bathed in light. Then the woman rose up in the air and disappeared. Filled with joy, the young man realized that he had been privileged to see the Mother of God, and he began to spread the word of his happy experience. The little shrine became a triumph of votive offerings. First the townspeople and later those from other regions began to come as pilgrims. A great swell of love and devotion to the Mother of God caused a reawakening of faith and piety. Conversions and contrite hearts multiplied, followed by a general reform of life in the area. The children were reconciled with the Father through Mary.

Although the image remained bright, through time the wall had begun to suffer from age and the weather. A crack as wide as a finger ran across the head of the Virgin in the picture. The wall seemed in imminent danger of collapse. A few days after the apparition seen by Sebastiano, the crack miraculously closed, leaving only a nearly invisible line as a sign of the prodigy.

As with every popular devotion in the church, that of Our Lady of the Garden attracted some who branded the devotion as superstition. An influential priest, Don Agostino Repetto, was the leader of opposition to the devotion. Based on his report, the vicar general of Genoa ordered the picture to be covered.

The people rose up in protest. In the parish of St. Giovanni, the Blessed Sacrament was exposed for three days while the people flocked to pray for the truth of the devotion to be shown. The city officials sent a representative to Genoa to ask for an ecclesiastical investigation. A tribunal was established, and the vicar general came to Chiavari on July 24, 1610. The night before the tribunal was to open, a young man named Lazzaro Caprino, who had been afflicted with a speech impediment since childhood, prayed fervently at the shrine for a cure. He passed out in front of the shrine, and on coming to, he was cured and able to speak normally. The following morning as Sebastiano Descalzo was testifying about his apparition, the examination was interrupted when the people carried Caprino in triumph to the vicar general to testify to the new miracle. There are records extant today of the testimony of Descalzo, Caprino, and others who had received favors and graces. The tribunal also investigated the miraculous closing of the crack. The process concluded that in forty-seven cases, there was divine intervention, and the devotion to Our Lady of the Garden received ecclesiastical approval. At the conclusion of the inquiry, the members of the tribunal and the vicar general, one of the most renowned theologians of his day, went to the garden in an act of public veneration on July 27, 1610.

A small chapel was built to protect the sacred image. Controversy continued, and a second investigation was instituted. Again, the decision was in favor of the devotion; and on May 25, 1612, the first solemn Mass was celebrated in the little chapel. Later, the former head of the opposition, Don Repetto, was among the celebrants.

In 1613, the cornerstone for a new church in honor of Our Lady of the Garden was set. The care of the shrine was given to the Carmelite Fathers in 1627, and the temple was completed and blessed in 1633. Today it is a basilica and the cathedral of the diocese. On September 8, 1634, the sacred image was detached from the wall, placed in a fitting frame, and carried in joyful procession to the church. The image was crowned in 1769. In 1904, Pope St. Pius X elevated the shrine to the dignity of Pontifical Minor Basilica.

Since the first favor granted to Geronima Turrio in favor of her seafaring son, the Madonna of the Garden seems to have displayed a predilection for the sailors of the world. In 1642, the town of Chiavari donated a warship to the navy of the Republic of Genoa. The ship was christened with the name of the town's patroness, Santa Maria dell'Orto. Soon, other ships began to be christened with her name, and her colors flew proudly on the flags of Liguria's merchant marine. The fame of Our Lady of the Garden spread to other ports. By 1481, a citizen of Genoa had built a church and a hospital in Rome for Ligurian sailors who were ill.

St. Anthony Gianelli (1789–1846) had a deep filial devotion to Our Lady of the Garden, and he consecrated himself and his people to her. He inspired three institutions which today continue to spread the devotion throughout the world. He was prefect of studies at the seminary of Chiavari, which is located next to the basilica. Through the story of the sacred image, he inspired the young clerics to imitate the virtues of Mary. The Congregation of the Missionaries of St. Alphonsus was established in 1827 to further the sanctification of the diocesan clergy by an annual retreat and to promote the preaching of missions to the people. Gianelli recommended the devotion to the missionaries, asking them to spread it in the parishes to which they would be called. In 1829, he began the Institute of the Daughters of Mary, Our Lady of the Garden, who even today continue to spread the devotion through their work in hospitals, schools, orphanages, and other social institutions throughout the world. The spread of the congregation is inexorably intertwined with the spread of veneration for Our Lady of the Garden.

The first printed pictures of Our Lady of the Garden go back to 1610. Copies of the image were made and distributed in all sizes. Little copies of the picture are still distributed by the sisters today.

In the areas that benefited from the charitable work of the sisters in South America, many children are given the name Maria del Huerta, in honor of Our Lady of the Garden. In Spanish, the name signifies not simply a garden but a fruitful one. In truth, devotion to Mary under this title is fruitful, inviting her devotee into the wonders of the divine love and mercy of our Father.

The feast of Our Lady of the Garden is celebrated on July 2, commemorating the apparition of Sebastiano Descalzo at the original shrine.

I attended Our Lady of the Garden school during my elementary, high school, and college years in the province of Salta, Argentina. Through the sisters, I learned the true devotion to the Blessed Mother. While at school, I went to visit the Virgin every day in her chapel, and talked with her as I do with my mother. She saw my tears many times, some-

*times because I was sad but more often when I was over-
whelmed with happiness. Our Lady knew all my problems
and concerns. When I grew up and left my blood family to
join the religious life, I felt as if I never lost my mother; her
presence is even stronger. She is still there guiding me in all
my decisions. As superior of the community, every day I offer
Our Lady of the Garden a rosary early in the morning asking her to mother the sisters under my care, because she
knows better their hearts and their needs. I know that she
does! I usually ask her for what I need, but sometimes she
will fulfill even my inner desires. She is truly my Mother.*

—Sister Inez Aparicio

Sister Inez Aparicio is a high
school teacher and superior of
the Sisters of Our Lady of the
Garden in Staten Island,
New York.

Prayer to Our Lady of the Garden

Our Lady of the Garden, my good and
loving Mother, cover me with your holy
mantle and give me your maternal blessing.

Sweet Mother of Den Bosch
's-Hertogenbosch, the Netherlands

Just like her fellow Dutch Catholics, the Sweet Mother of Den Bosch has survived some rough times. Through the years, however, the love of the Sweet Lady has remained a constant in the hearts of her subjects, both in her native land and abroad.

Three and a half feet tall, the carved oak image depicts Our Lady with the Christ Child on her left arm. The artist and the first years of the statue are unknown. Her recorded history begins one cold day in 1380. A workman at the church of St. Jan was looking for wood for a fire when he discovered an old statue in a workshop near the church. Since the statue apparently had been abandoned for years, he decided to use it to kindle his fire.

The master of the shop, seeing the imminent desecration, rescued the statue and gave it to a certain Brother Wouter, who was given permission to take it to his room for private devotion. According to ancient legend, as he carried the statue, it became so heavy that he could move it no farther than the church, where he placed it on the altar of the sodality of Our Lady. Immediately, a flood of graces flowed out from the image, and the church became a place of pilgrimage to the Sweet Mother.

Art historians believe the statue was probably carved between 1280 and 1320. The image was painted in 1481, with prominent colors of red, green, and gold, at the suggestion of Emperor Maximillian. It was before the newly painted image that the emperor witnessed the induction of his three-year-old son, Philip the Handsome, into the Order of the Golden Fleece.

The cathedral of St. Jan (John) was begun as the parish church of the town in the early thirteenth century and was dedicated to St. John the Evangelist. Construction of the Gothic church began around 1380. It was raised to cathedral status in 1561. St. Jan is the most important example of Gothic architecture in the northern Netherlands and one of the few medieval churches of this size in the area that is now used for Catholic services. (Most of the others remained Protestant after the restoration of the episcopal hierarchy in the Netherlands in the nineteenth century.)

Our Lady's chapel, where the image stands today, looks much

the same as it did in the fourteenth century. For eleven months of the year, the statue of Our Sweet Mother of Den Bosch reigns from a cream-colored, circular pedestal in the Lady Chapel, surrounded by candles, flowers, and votive offerings. During the Marian month of May, the image is moved to the northern nave to receive the thousands of pilgrims who come to venerate her. The fraternity of Our Sweet Lady has taken care of the statue, the shrine, and its activities since 1837.

The Sweet Mother's home is in the Dutch city of 's-Hertogenbosch. When the United Kingdom of the Netherlands was proclaimed in 1815, 's-Hertogenbosch became the capital of the province of Northern Brabant.

The town itself was established in 1185, when the Duke of Braband gave city rights to a settlement near his hunting lodge in the middle of a wooded area. Our Lady's official title is the Sweet Mother of 's-Hertogenbosch, which means "from the duke's woods." Remains of the medieval city walls, earth ramparts, and bastions, built to protect the town, can still be seen today. Until the middle of the sixteenth century, 's-Hertogenbosch thrived, remaining under Spanish domination much longer than most other Dutch cities. During this time, the image began to be dressed in sumptuous robes in the Spanish style.

A sodality, the Brotherhood of Our Lady, cared for the image, her altar, and chapel, and arranged the annual processions. One of the brotherhood's most famous members was the artist Hieronymus (or Jeroen) Bosch, who took his name from the town. Van Aken was his family name. The most extravagant painter of his time, Bosch's pictures have always fascinated viewers. For some he seems a sort of fifteenth-century surrealist; others think his art reflects mysterious practices of the Middle Ages.

In 1486–87, Bosch's name appears for the first time in the membership lists of the Brotherhood of Our Lady, with which he was closely associated for the rest of his life. One of many sodalities dedicated to the Virgin, the Brotherhood of Our Lady of 'sHertogenbosch was a large and wealthy organization. They commissioned works of art to embellish the chapel of Our Lady.

Bosch was responsible for designing some of the stained-glass windows, among other items. He painted several altarpieces for the cathedral, all of which are now lost. An entry in the accounts of the brotherhood records Bosch's death in 1516.

About the middle of the sixteenth century, the town began to be afflicted with the religious problems of the Reformation. In 1566 the town suffered the Beeldenstorm, the full force of the iconoclastic fury. A group of fanatics pillaged the cathedral, breaking windows and smashing statues. Miraculously, the image of the Sweet Mother survived that attack.

In 1629, the city was conquered by Prince Frederik Hendrik, and St. Jan fell into Protestant hands and went into use for Dutch Reformed church services. The Catholic faith was forbidden in the Netherlands, and during these difficult times, sturdy Catholics risked their lives to keep the faith. Mass was celebrated secretly in barns, cellars, and sheds. These were known as *Schuilkerken* (secret churches).

Her pious devotees secretly smuggled their Sweet Mother to safety in Belgium. She was taken first to Antwerp and then to Brussels, where she remained for more than two hundred years in the Coudenberg church. Here, many pilgrims visited her, including some of her faithful subjects from Den Bosch.

At last, when Napoleon Bonaparte arrived, things began to change. He ordered the return of the cathedral to the Catholics in 1810, but by this time the area had been under Protestant domination for so long that it was considered mission territory and no bishop was appointed until 1853. In that year, at last, the Sweet Mother returned home to her people.

An annual jubilee each July celebrates the Sweet Mother's return to Den Bosch. In 1878, the statue was crowned by approval of Pope Leo XIII, shortly after his election. A Mass under the title of the Sweet Mother was approved by Pope Pius X in 1903, and in 1929 the cathedral was given the status of basilica by Pope Pius XI. The feast of the Sweet Mother is July 7, and from the 7th through the 15th, she is carried around in an annual procession known as the *Omgang,* or "going round." A pious legend holds that she marked the route herself during the plague when she descended from the throne and visited the people in their distress.

In 2003, the diocese celebrated the 150th anniversary of the Sweet Mother's return from Belgium. A number of special events were held, including an exhibit at the local museum. During the exhibition, many items concerning the Sweet Lady were displayed, including the "Miracle Book," which contains the records of favors and miracles attributed to her intercession from the fourteenth through the seventeenth centuries.

In 1921, the power of the Sweet Lady's beneficent aid was felt in the United States. In the records of the shrine at Den Bosch, there is mention that

> a certain Florence de Pauw, the daughter of the maid of Ch. Franken, parish priest of Kewanee, Illinois, was cured after her husband, her mother, and the priest held a novena in honor of the Sweet Lady of Den Bosch. Florence was having such a terrible pregnancy that the doctors had given up hope of a successful delivery. However, after the novena had been prayed, Florence gave birth to a healthy son on the 6th of November 1921. Both mother and son survived the delivery. According to Father Frenken, who sent a letter to a Dutch newspaper, it was owing to the Sweet Lady that the mother and her child were saved.

The original Catholic Dutch colonists came to the United States about 1848 when a large group came with a Dutch Dominican priest and settled in the Fox River Valley area of Wisconsin. In 1907, a league of Holland and Belgian priests was organized in Chicago for the twofold purpose of providing for the spiritual needs of neglected Dutch and Belgian Catholics and of helping their countrymen on their arrival in America. Father Charles Frenken was sent to St. Joseph's parish in Kewanee, Illinois, in 1912, to minister to the Belgian and Dutch parishioners.

In time of trouble, no doubt he, like so many of her clients, turned naturally to ask the aid of the Sweet Mother.

For me, the Sweet Lady of Den Bosch is a symbol of religious freedom in my country. She survived the religious problems of Dutch history. Due to the intolerance of Protestant iconoclasts, she had to flee her country in the seventeenth century. However, when the Sweet Lady made her return more than two hundred years later, the Netherlands had evolved from a society where anything that was not Protestant was oppressed to a multireligious nation where Protestants, Catholics, Jews, and people from other faiths live peacefully together. This makes the history of the Sweet Lady of Den Bosch still relevant today; she is not merely an icon of medieval Catholicism but a survivor of a turbulent national history and a superhuman presence that still means as much to her devotees as she did almost seven hundred years ago.

—Pieter van den Bos

Pieter van den Bos received his master's degree in communication science from the University of Amsterdam. Pieter lives in The Hague and is working as a postman while he is looking for the "right" job.

Our Lady of Aberdeen
Aberdeen, Scotland

Since the Reformation, Scotland has been known as a Protestant country. The "old faith," and a deep devotion to the Virgin Mary, still lives in the minds and hearts of today's Scottish Catholics.

The only known devotional statue to have survived from the pre-Reformation Scottish Church is a small wooden image of Our Lady and her Divine Child that now stands in Brussels, Belgium. It is known to the people there as Notre Dame du Bon Succes. The French title of the image originates from a victory of the Spanish Infanta in a battle against the "Hollanders" on the day that the ship carrying the image arrived at Ostend.

Scottish Catholics know her by another name: Our Lady of Aberdeen. Even though absent from her native land, she is still venerated under this title by her sturdy Scottish subjects.

For sixty-five perilous years, from 1560 to 1625, the Catholic Church in Scotland was persecuted. The image of Our Lady was successfully hidden by a faithful Scottish family until it was sent to safety in Belgium.

The statue is of carved wood, executed in the Flemish style of the late fifteenth century. She holds the Infant Jesus on her arm, and there is a silver scepter in her hand. Mother and Child wear silver crowns, which are probably replacements for the originals.

The statue originally stood in the bishop's castle adjoining the medieval cathedral of Aberdeen. Tradition associates it with the holy bishop Gavin Dunbar (d. ca. 1531). Dunbar was one of the builders of St. Machar's Cathedral, and he provided the inspiration for its unique painted ceiling. Pious legend holds that the image of Our Lady spoke to him, telling him where to build the magnificent bridge over the river Dee, which was formally opened in 1527 and which, restored and widened, still stands today with its original sixteenth-century piers, coats of arms, and passing places.

In 1559, when the Reformers began to make headway in Aberdeen, Bishop William Gordon removed the sacred images and valuable items from the cathedral and confided them to others for safety. The plate and chalices were given to the care of the prebendaries, or canons, of the church. A beautiful silver Madonna that stood in the cathedral was given to one of the canons and has been lost to history.

The sacred vestments and other items were placed in the care of the earl of Huntly, George Gordon, the bishop's nephew, who gave his bond to return them to the church at a later and safer time. The earl, known as the "Cock of the North," was a devout Catholic. He took the sacred items and hid them at his palace, Strathbogie at Huntly, Aberdeenshire, in the northeast of the country. Gordon's palace was sacked in 1562, and the rich vestments from Aberdeen Cathedral were taken away to Holyrood, but no mention is made of the appropriation of other articles of Catholic worship.

The sixth earl of Huntly, grandson of the original and also named George, led an exciting life. He was convicted of high treason, fled to France for three years, and eventually returned to the favor of King James VI and was named the first marquis of Scotland. The ancestral castle of Strathbogie was embellished with even greater splendor than before. Inside its walls was a chapel of the Blessed Virgin Mary where the marquis, his devout wife, Henrietta Stewart, their family, and faithful servants assisted at Mass celebrated by fugitive priests. The Jesuit martyr St. John Ogilvie spent the Christmas of 1613 at Strathbogie. Although there is no historical evidence as proof, it is likely that he prayed in the presence of the little wooden Virgin of Aberdeen. It is without doubt, however, that his devotion to the Mother of Our Lord was deep.

A native of Scotland, John Ogilvie was brought up a Calvinist, but he converted to the faith in his teens while traveling on the continent. He joined the Jesuits and was ordained in Paris at age thirty. Three years later, he returned to minister to his persecuted countrymen disguised as a horse dealer with the name of John Watson. His missionary activities were brief but fruitful; then he was betrayed and imprisoned. While he was in prison, he was able to write about his imprisonment and torture; and he smuggled the story out, page by page, to his Jesuit superiors through the kindness of visitors to other prisoners. Eventually found guilty of high treason, he was sentenced to be hanged and quartered. In spite of sickness and harsh treatment and torture, he kept a quick, often sharp, wit, high spirits, and a deep devotion to Our Lady, carrying her beads as a symbol of his faith as he walked to his execution. Although commanded not to address the crowd gathered to witness his death, when the minister announced that the execution was for treason not religion, John quietly objected. Even at the hour of his death, he was able to outwit his adversary. In the brief exchange with the minister, he convinced him to announce to the crowd: "I promise Mr. Ogilvie his life, the archbishop's daughter in marriage, and a very rich living, provided he will come over to our side."

"Then there is no fear that I shall be guilty of treason hereafter?" asked the prisoner.

"None at all," replied the minister.

"So I stand here a criminal for the cause of religion alone?"

The crowd drew the conclusion that the minister had not foreseen and shouted, "For that alone!"

"Very well," said Ogilvie, now addressing the spectators, "and for that I would happily give life many times over. Take the one that I have, and do not delay—for you shall never take my religion from me."

As the officers came to bind his hands, the valiant young priest threw his rosary into the crowd. It struck a young Hungarian nobleman, Jean de Eckersdorff, on the chest. He later became a Catholic and attributed his conversion to the martyr's rosary. As Ogilvie was hanged by his neck, an executioner pulled on his feet to end the pain. The quartering ordered by the sentence of execution was not carried out.

The persecution of Catholics continued, yet devotion to Our Blessed Lady remained among the people and was fostered by the zealous, hidden, and wandering priests.

In 1625, the marquis and his wife, now elderly, considered themselves obliged in some way to fulfill the sacred promise made by the fourth earl in 1599 to return the property of the cathedral to the church. The vestments had long since been carried off, and there was little left except the ancient and revered statue of the Virgin. The Scottish cathedral had been desecrated, and the chapter disbanded. The persecutions were intensified, and the iconoclasts were determined to destroy any venerable relic of Catholic times. To continue to attempt to hide the image would imperil its preservation. To them, the best solution would be to send it abroad secretly to the Spanish archduchess Clara Isabella Eugenia, regent of the Spanish Netherlands. Perhaps they had a premonition, for within only a few years the sacred emblems of Our Lord over the doorway of their palace felt the steel of the chisel of the anti-Catholic army of the Covenant, their son was beheaded, and their grandson forced to flee, as the family home began its steady slide into decay.

Secret arrangements were made with a merchant, and the statue was put aboard a Spanish ship and taken to the archduchess, who would treasure the little image in her palace at Brussels. The very secrecy of the voyage led to a pious belief that the statue was thrown into the sea at Aberdeen and carried on the waves miraculously to Ostend.

The ship arrived safely, and the Scottish Madonna was placed in the chapel of the palace in Brussels. The archduchess's chaplain, Father de los Rios, petitioned the regent to give the image to the newly built Augustinian church in Brussels, and in 1626 it was taken there in solemn procession. The little Madonna remained there until 1796, when Our Lady once again had to go into hiding.

The French Revolution rumbled throughout Europe, and the Augustinians, fearing for the safety of their beloved image of the Madonna, gave it for safekeeping to an English resident in Brussels, John Baptist Joseph Morris, who concealed it successfully until 1805, when it was restored to its original shrine.

In 1814, when the Augustinians lost custody of the church, Our Lady was transferred to the parish church of Finistere, where in 1852 a special chapel was built to enshrine the image. Here she is venerated by her Belgian devotees as Notre Dame du Bon Succes, and by the occasional Scottish visitor as Our Lady of Aberdeen.

In 1895, the Mesdames of the Sacred Heart established a foundation in Roehampton, London. Influenced by a devout Scottish priest, they took up the devotion to Our Lady of Aberdeen and promoted it in many ways. In 1895, a group of religious was sent from Roehampton to Aberdeen to make a new foundation at 3 Queen's Cross. When the first sisters arrived at the new convent, they were met by a beautiful replica of the image of Our Lady of Aberdeen that had been commissioned by Reverend Mother Mabel Digby. Official approbation was later given to Our Lady of Aberdeen as Our Lady of Good Succor, and her feast is celebrated on July 9.

A number of early attempts were made to bring the original image back to Scotland. Shortly after World War I, a group of Scottish highlanders planned to kidnap the image, but when they saw the great devotion of her Belgian clients, they abandoned their plans and joined in the prayers at her shrine.

The devotion to her as Our Lady of Aberdeen has not waned but increased. In the Holy Year of 1975, an exact replica of the image made a prayerful journey, under the auspices of the Knights of St. Columba, from St. Mary's Cathedral, Aberdeen, to Westminster Cathedral, London.

There is a replica of the statue in a chapel at the rear of St. Mary's Cathedral in Huntly Street, Aberdeen.

The Aberdeen title of Our Lady brings to my mind all that the good sisters taught me in school when I was a boy. They instilled in me, by their word and example, a deep devotion to the Mother of God. That devotion to Our Lady of Aberdeen rises in my heart and soul and makes me proud of the faith of my forefathers. I think Dante, in his Paradiso, Canto XXXIII, encapsulates what every Catholic heart truly feels in St. Bernard's prayer to the Virgin:

*"Lady, so great thou art and such thy might
the seeker after grace, who shuns thy knee,
may aim his prayer but fails to wing the flight."*

—Michael Skelly

Michael Skelly is a retired local government housing officer. His home town is Dundee, but he is now happily living in retirement in Edinburgh, Scotland.

Our Lady of the Hmong People
Fresno, California

An unusual and attractive little image of Mary stands serenely on a small altar in St. Mary's Church in Fresno, California. Carved from wood, Our Lady is painted wearing traditional Hmong clothing. The statue is a gift from Hmong parishioners.

Standing only twelve inches high, the image is dressed in a white robe with a blue mantle painted to symbolize Hmong needlework, called *Pa Ntaub*, with a light tan yoke. A red and green sash circles the Virgin's waist. The headpiece is royal purple with black-and-white stripes. Mary wears a traditional silver necklace and earrings and carries a rosary over her arm.

The statue was carved and painted by the sculptor Manuel Rodriguez, who is a parishioner of the church. Rodriguez worked with another parishioner, Tzer Lee Thao, who furnished him pictures of traditional Hmong clothing and designs and who consulted with him about the clothing of the statue. The lovely little image stands as a welcome to, and in solidarity with, her Hmong children.

Monsignor Patrick McCormick, the pastor of St. Mary's, serves a multicultural parish. In the year 2000, he asked representatives of the largest cultural groups to have an image of Our Lady made to represent their culture. The Hmong image was completed and presented to the church in 2002; it was blessed on December 14. During a New Year's celebration in 2003, the community announced that the statue was to represent all of the Hmong people, not just those of St. Mary's Church.

America owes a great debt of gratitude to the Hmong people from Laos. While serving in special guerrilla units during the Vietnam War, Hmong soldiers rescued many American pilots who were shot down over Laos. Most of the combat forces on the ground in Laos were Hmong, who cut off the supplies to the North Vietnamese as they traveled south along the Ho Chi Minh trail. By the time America pulled out of Vietnam, thousands of Hmong men, women, and children had been killed, and more than 100,000 fled to Thai refugee camps. Thousands died while crossing the jungles and the Mekong River. A long genocidal campaign against the Hmong has been conducted by the Laotian and

Vietnamese governments in vengeance for Hmong support of the United States during the war.

The Hmong people came originally from several southern provinces of mainland China. In the middle of the nineteenth century, thousands of Hmong migrated to the highlands of North Vietnam, Laos, and Thailand.

By 1975, there were about 250,000 of these hill people in Laos. For more than three decades, the Hmong who lived in Laos fought the Vietnamese Communists. Between 1976 and 1985, thousands of Hmong came to the United States. They were recognized as refugees because of the sacrifice made by Hmong soldiers who fought as U.S. allies. Most of them entered the country with nothing more than the clothes on their backs.

Today, there are over 150,000 Hmong people in the United States, most of whom settled in Wisconsin, Minnesota, and California. There are also large Hmong communities in the Carolinas, Georgia, Massachusetts, and Rhode Island. Several million Hmong people remain in China, Thailand, and Laos.

Only a small percent of Hmong are Catholic. Unlike some other Asian nations who have a history in the church that extends back over three hundred years, the Hmong are possibly the youngest star in the galaxy of the Catholic Church. The first Hmong baptism in Laos took place in 1954. Catholic Hmong communities have been in China for more than eighty years and have been able to keep their faith alive, even under the Communist regime. Father Tito Banchong is the first Hmong priest of the Hmong Lao. He is now a bishop for the diocese of Luangphrabang in Laos. Father Banchong has gone through many persecutions and survived. He is a living witness of the faith.

The only native Hmong priest in the United States, and one of only four known Hmong priests in the world, is Father Chue Ying Vang, who was ordained in May 1992 in the Minneapolis-St. Paul archdiocese. Father Vang came to the United States in 1980 at the age of sixteen, and first settled in Rochester, Minnesota. He attended St. Paul Seminary.

Father Daniel Taillez, O.M.I., sees Father Vang's ordination as "a very positive sign for Hmong Catholics." Father Taillez, worked as a missionary in Laos until 1974, when the Communists expelled him from the country. He continues his missionary work among the Hmong and the Laotian people, working to keep the communities together and to develop programs for ongoing training of lay leaders. The Hmong Catholics minister to one another. They gather regularly in rosary and prayer groups to nourish their faith and spirituality.

Father Anthony McGuire, director of the Office of Pastoral Care for Migrants and Refugees, an arm of the Catholic Bishops' Conference Office of Migration and Refugee Services, writes,

> Their church life could be compared to the Christians in the generation right after the Apostles—a small but dedicated community struggling to incorporate their faith in Jesus and the teachings of the Church into their Hmong culture, and discerning how to evangelize others in their community. Lay Catechists are a key group in this fledgling community.

The Hmong come from an agrarian culture whose religious beliefs are based in animism. Although the youth have blended into American society exceptionally well, it has been a continuing struggle for the older people because of problems with language and cultural differences. The Hmong culture contains some customs, such as the early age for marriage, that are problematic in contemporary American society. The Hmong language, folktales, and traditions were passed along to each generation by word of mouth for thousands of years. It was not until late in the twentieth century that a writing system for the Hmong language was introduced by Christian missionaries in the country. Father Yves Bertrais, O.M.I., was the first missionary to the Hmong. With the help of a Protestant missionary and a linguist, he invented the Hmong romanized aphabet. Father Bertrais is now in Thailand doing a Hmong program for Radio Veritas Asia.

There were few schools in the mountains of Laos, so most of the older immigrants came to this country without being able to read or write. Fiercely independent and highly motivated, today's young Hmong are graduating from high school and entering college. In the fewer than thirty years they have been in this country, there is already a core band of professionals and successful businessmen. One study of six Wisconsin public school districts showed that Hmong students consistently performed above the national norms on standardized tests. These students have an astounding graduation rate of 95 percent. In spite of their own limited education, Hmong parents recognize and actively support the value of education for their children.

The Catholic Church has been a key player in the resettlement and assimilation to life in America for the thousands of immigrants from Southeast Asia. The United States Catholic Conference and Catholic Charities help to resettle refugees regardless of their religious affiliation. For those who are Catholic, however, dioceses try to provide a parish life that will be respectful of their language and culture.

In Fresno, California, Our Lady of the Hmong People welcomes her son's people with more than just the exterior clothing of the image. Like them, she also knew the suffering of being a refugee from her own land. With the tender heart of a mother she seems to say, "Come, and be Hmong and U.S. American. Do not fear, I am here with you."

I have a special devotion to Mary and am amazed by her great love and faithfulness. She must have had a special love for God that the Word became flesh in her womb. Mary was not free from trouble: the thought of divorce quietly by her husband (Matthew 1:19), the flight to Egypt (Matthew 1:13), the loss of her Child Jesus in the temple (Luke 2:41–51), and the crucifixion and death of her son on the cross (John 19:26). In spite of her troubles, she remained faithful and believed that what God promised to her would

be fulfilled. Mary is a mother who is very close to her children. She knows each of them. She is a perfect model for priests and for all who wish to dedicate themselves to God.
—Rev. Chue Ying Vang

Father Chue is the first Hmong priest ordained in the United States.

Our Lady of Guadalupe of Los Angeles
Los Angeles, California

The Mother of the Americas is a perfect description of this representation of Our Lady of Guadalupe. Although the likeness is particular to the indigenous people of Mexico, she stands as a mother to all and for all. This became very apparent during the "Tilma of Tepeyac" tour of 2003. I will always remember that this statue and relic seemed to create a renaissance within the Catholic Church across America.

—Tom Serafin

Tom Serafin is president of a lay apostolate to promote the proper veneration of relics. He is the author of the book *Relics, the Forgotten Sacramental.*

To read more about Our Lady of Guadalupe of Los Angeles, please visit the special section "Other Faces of Mary" on the author's website: www.annball.com.

Our Lady of the Atocha
Fresnillo, Zacatecas, Mexico—Toledo, Spain

Although many Catholics are familiar with the miracle-working little image known as Santo Niño de Atocha, most do not realize that the devotion begins with devotion to Mary under her title Our Lady of Atocha.

The prayers and novenas to the little pilgrim image of the Christ Child all begin with prayers to his mother. Because Jesus is shown as a small child, his clients first ask his mother's permission for him to go to their aid. As in all true Marian devotions, the Holy Virgin is begged for her intercession with her son.

The image in Mexico portrays Mary as a fair-skinned medieval Spanish queen dressed in richly embroidered clothing with a lace mantilla and a golden crown. In her right hand she holds a golden rose. Her Divine Son usually rests on her left arm. Dressed as a Spanish pilgrim, the child has Indian features. This image is a true pilgrim and often leaves the church in Zacatecas to travel to other cities, both in Mexico and in the United States. Those of Mexican heritage have a saying about him: "El Santo Niño mueve corazones" (the Holy Child moves hearts).

Tradition says devotion to Our Lady of Atocha originated in Antioch, and that St. Luke the Evangelist was the sculptor of the first mother-and-child image. Thus, Atocha could be a corruption of Antiochia. The devotion spread rapidly, and by 1162, it reached Spain. A carved wood statue of Our Lady of Atocha was in the Church of St. Leocadia in Toledo, and in 1523, Charles V of Spain built an enormous temple and placed the statue under the care of the Dominicans. The image of the Divine Child was detachable, and devout families would borrow the image of the infant when a woman was about to give birth to her child.

The legend of the miraculous nature of the statue originates from the dark years of the Moorish invaders. The Spanish Catholics were persecuted, and in Atocha, a suburb of Madrid, many were thrown into Moorish dungeons. The Moors did not feed their prisoners, so food had to be brought by their families. During one period of persecution, the caliph ordered that no one over the age of twelve would be allowed to go into the prisons to take food. Men who had no young relatives would starve.

The women of the town went to the parish church and appealed to the Virgin for help. Soon the children of the town came home with an interesting story. An unknown young boy was visiting the prisoners and feeding them. He came at night, slipping past the sleeping guards, and the little water gourd he carried held enough to slake the thirst of all. His little bread basket remained full, no matter how much bread he distributed to the hungry prisoners.

Those who had asked the Virgin of Atocha for a miracle began to suspect the identity of the little boy. As if in confirmation, the shoes on the image seemed to be worn out. When they replaced the shoes with new ones, these, too, seemed to wear out quickly.

After Ferdinand and Isabella drove the Moors from Spain in

1492, the people continued to invoke the aid of Our Lady and her Holy Child. They asked help in particular for those who were in jail and those who were "imprisoned" in the mines. When the Spaniards came to the New World, they brought along the devotions of their native regions. In 1540, silver mines were established in the northern area of Mexico, and mineworkers from Madrid brought their devotion to Our Lady and her miracle-working, pilgrim infant. In Plateros, a tiny village near the mines of Fresnillo, a church in honor of El Niño de Santa María de Atocha became a major place of pilgrimage. Here the Holy Child continued his miracle working for those who appealed to him through his mother.

The original statue for this church, made as a duplicate of the one in Spain, was donated by a rich mine owner. It, too, had a removable infant which could be borrowed. At one time, the image of the child was lost, and when the replacement was carved the new babe had Indian features.

Through a century of revolution, Mexico has provided many prisoners for the Holy Child to aid. Annually, other miraculous cures and escapes are reported here. A special building had to be built near the church to hold all the *ex voto* offerings brought to the Holy Child.

As the cult began to spread in the mid-nineteenth century, it became more Christological and less Marian. At the shrine in Chimayo, New Mexico, there is no image of Our Lady, although prayers still begin with an appeal to Our Lady of Atocha. Here the Holy Child acquired another patronage—the military. Some of the first American troops to see action in World War II were from the New Mexico National Guard. They fought bravely in the underground tunnels and defenses of Corregidor. The Catholics remembered that the Santo Niño de Atocha had long been considered a patron of all who were trapped or imprisoned. Many of them made a vow that if they survived the war, they would make a pilgrimage from Santa Fe to Chimayo in thanksgiving. At the end of the war, a large group of veterans of Corregidor, the Bataan death march, and Japanese prison camps, together with their families, walked the long and rough road from Santa Fe to Chimayo, some walking barefoot over the rocky ground to the little adobe shrine.

During the recent Gulf War, American mothers begged for help for their children. A visitor to the shrine at Fresnillo today will see many photographs of United States military personnel left as *ex votos* in thanks to Santo Niño de Atocha and his serene mother, Our Lady of Atocha.

Dear Mother, thank you very much for letting your Son help me. You and He have taken care of me twice while going off to war and kept me from harm twice. Too often, we forget our manners in not saying "thank you" enough to the creator of such a beautiful life. Being the mother of an only son myself, I know how hard it can be to share your child. Thank you for taking care of me while I was gone and watching over my child and others I love. In His name I pray.

—Joanna Ball

Joanna Ball is a Tech Sergeant in the United States Air Force. Career military, she is currently stationed in Mississippi.

Our Lady of Africa
Algiers, Algeria

Charles Cardinal Lavigerie (1825–92) was a man of extraor-
dinary vision and foresight, unique in his time. Named as the first
archbishop of Algiers in 1867, he hoped and dreamed for the
material, intellectual, and spiritual development of the peoples of
Africa. In 1868 and 1869 respectively, he founded two mission-

ary congregations, whose dedicated apostolic work has borne good fruit for the continent.

Born at Bayonne, France, in 1825, Charles Lavigerie was ordained in 1849. After a number of appointments, he was consecrated bishop of Nancy (1863) and became a trusted advisor to Pope Leo XIII. He was an active participant in many of the affairs of the church, proposing a respectful approach to the churches of the oriental tradition and rejecting a narrow view of religion. He joyfully accepted the appointment to Algiers as opening a door to the spread of the gospel in Africa.

At a time when European colonization was imposing a Western culture on Africa and exploiting its resources while keeping silent about the heinous slave trade, Charles Lavigerie, a man with an open mind, longed for a universal church that would be adapted to the times and close to the people. Lavigerie struggled against war, famine, and injustice, and campaigned against the slave trade. In a speech in 1888, he spoke these memorable words: "I am a man and nothing that is human is indifferent to me. I am a man; an injustice against another human being revolts my heart. I am a man and that which I would like done to me, I want to do for others."

Lavigerie urged his missionaries to put themselves entirely at the service of Africa and its people, telling them, "Be apostles, be nothing but apostles." He insisted that they study and speak the language of the African people among whom they were living, calling on them to become international communities. He stressed education, and sent young Africans to study in Europe so they could return as doctor catechists to their African homes.

In 1873, Cardinal Lavigerie transferred a beautiful statue of Our Lady to the new Church of Our Lady of Africa in Algiers. Known as Our Lady of Africa, the bronze image is very dark in color but with European features. The image portrays the Virgin with her hands outstretched, standing on a globe with her foot crushing a serpent. Just under four feet in height, the front of the globe carries the inscription *"Virgo Fidelis"* (faithful virgin).

The construction of the church in Algiers had been begun

under Bishop Pavy, and was completed and consecrated in 1872 by Bishop Lavigerie. In April of 1876 the image was crowned by the authority of Pope Pius IX, and the church was raised to the status of basilica. The same pontiff granted an indulgence to all the faithful who would visit the church and pray before the statue on the anniversary of the crowning, April 30th. At the annual feast, and other times during the year, many Muslims, as well as her Catholic children, come to venerate Our Lady, just as they do at other shrines of Our Lady in North Africa.

The Algiers image in the Basilica of Notre Dame of Africa is a copy of a copy of an eighteenth-century image sculpted in silver, in the grand style of the artists of Louis XIV's reign, at St. Sulpice by the French artist Edmé Bouchardon. A hundred years later, in 1838, the archbishop of Paris had two copies made in bronze as tokens of thanksgiving for the conversion of ex-bishop Talleyrand, who had left the priesthood during the French Revolution. One copy was given to the Ladies of the Sacred Heart (now called the Religious of the Sacred Heart) in Paris. In 1839, the first bishop of Algiers, Bishop Dupuch, went to France to find priests and other resources for his new diocese. Visiting Lyons in 1840, he gave a talk to the Children of Mary at La Ferrandière about the missions. The confraternity promised him a statue of Our Lady and suggested that he order one that pleased him. On seeing the image at the house of the Ladies of the Sacred Heart, he chose it, and a copy was made and presented to him. It is this copy that is known today as Our Lady of Africa.

On his return to Algiers, the bishop kept the image for a time on the terrace of his residence. It was later lent to the Trappists of Staoueli. Bishop Dupuch's successor, Bishop Pavy, had it moved to two temporary chapels before it was placed in what would become the Basilica of Our lady of Africa.

In 1886, the image was dressed in a beautiful embroidered gown, the gift of a devotee and with the donations of many of the faithful. The gown was replaced and Our Lady was reclothed in special ceremonies in 1925, 1950, and most recently in 1985. Today the image wears a blue-and-white dress and robe embroidered in the traditional Algerian technique known as *medjdoub*, which comes from an Arabic word meaning "to pull." The motifs are cut from thin leather and laid over velvet. They are then covered with gold threads that do not penetrate the cloth. On the inside, a linen thread pulls the gold threads, attaching them to both sides of the leather.

Adorned with the beautiful work of artists of her country, Our Lady of Africa stands regally to bless the people who come to venerate her.

Some pilgrims leave engraved stones as offerings at Our Lady's shrine. In 1967. Frank Borman, one of the first American astronauts to go to the moon, left an engraved stone in the basilica in memory of his pilgrimage.

> *Cardinal Lavigerie, the founder of our congregation (Missionary Sisters of Our Lady of Africa) wanted us missionaries to use the prayer to Our Lady of Africa as a "common weapon to touch and move the heart of Our Lord in favor of the apostolate." Since its beginnings, our congregation was placed under the protection of Our Lady of Africa. Each sister's devotion to her—and so is mine—is embedded in the devotion of the entire congregation. They are inseparable. However, we shall be glad if—through this book—many will get to know Our Lady of Africa and to pray to her for the people of Africa in their struggles and afflictions.*
>
> —Sister Hildegunde Schmidt

Sister Hildegunde is a member of the Missionary Sisters of Our Lady of Africa who works in the archives of her congregation in Rome. Originally from Germany, she had been a missionary in Zambia (central Africa) for twenty-four years before taking up her appointment in the Generalate.

Procession with Image of Our Lady of Africa,
Navrongo, Ghana

Prayer to Our Lady of Africa

Our Lady of Africa
Mother of Jesus and Our Mother,
Remember all the peoples of Africa.

You were present with the Apostles
at the beginning of the Church.
Be with the apostles of today
that they may proclaim
the Good News of Jesus Christ, your Son.

Help us to know and love Jesus.
Help us to follow Him faithfully.
Help us to care for one another.

Our Lady of Africa,
May your Son, Jesus Christ,
choose and send new missionaries
to Africa and to the whole world.

Our Lady of Penrhys
Rhondda Valley, South Wales

"Mary, mother of Christ, most renowned of maidens,
In thy great mercy intercede with thy Son
To drive our sins from us."
　　　　—from *The Black Book of Carmarthen.*

Before the Protestant Reformation, the Welsh countryside was blanketed with shrines and holy wells dedicated to the Virgin Mary. The principal medieval shrine was at Penrhys, in a grange, or outlying property, of the Cistercian Abbey of Llantarnam. The fame of this shrine and the miraculous image there, which showered graces and miracles of healing on devout pilgrims, reached far beyond the borders of the country.

Situated on a hilltop on a wooded slope near an oak forest, there was a sanctuary where the image of Our Lady was enthroned. As one Welsh poet wrote, "there the soul's pardon may be gained in the glade of Mary's five joys." Welsh poets of the Middle Ages sang of the crowds of pilgrims and the beauty of the image of Our Lady, "nursing Jesus with a kiss."

The history of the shrine of Penrhys is one of glory and defeat, of prayers and of final triumph over adversity. Today, in the heart of South Wales, the beauty of devotion to the Mother of God still burns brightly.

During the Reformation, at the dissolution of the monasteries, the beautiful image of Our Lady of Penrhys was captured, taken to London, and burned, at the same time as the famous images of Our lady of Walsingham and Ipswich were destroyed.

Four hundred years later, in 1939, the remains of the ancient sanctuary were given to the Catholic Archdiocese of Cardiff, a new stone statue was erected, and Mary's devotees once again began to venerate their beloved mother. The church at nearby Ferndale is dedicated to Our Lady of Penrhys, and a new image of her is located there.

The Cistercian Abbey at Llantarnam was founded in Monmouthshire in 1179. In 1205, the land at Penrhys was recognized as belonging to the abbey, and a grange, or substation, was built there, where farmland was cultivated and herds of sheep were tended. Monks from the abbey rotated to work at the grange, and a chapel was built for their spiritual exercises.

As is common with many shrines, there was a spring of water which gained renown for its healing powers. Possibly a pagan cult existed there before the coming of the faith, and the first missionaries "baptized" the water for Christian use. Legend holds that the original image of Our Lady of Penrhys was found in an oak tree near the well which was dedicated to the Virgin. News of the miraculous appearance of the statue spread, and crowds began to come to see the prodigy. The image was enshrined in Mary's church on top of the mountain, just above the holy well.

Penrhys soon developed into the greatest center of devotion to the Virgin in Wales, and pilgrims began arriving in a spirit of faith, devotion, and penance. They came from all social classes, including lords and fine ladies, although the majority were of the working class. At first they came from nearby areas; but as the fame of the shrine developed, they came from farther away. A hostel or guest house was built, and the monks, in addition to working at their farming duties, began to provide for the spiritual and material needs of the pilgrims.

A wealth of medieval writings is extant and gives a clue to the ordinary way of life of the times. Pilgrims often came in a spirit of penance, walking on their knees and carrying candles. The literature tells of fasting and other penitential practices, including nighttime vigils, baths in the healing waters of the well, and the offerings from grateful devotees at the shrine. The summer, especially during the feast of the Assumption, was the most popular time for pilgrimages. A constant refrain in the poets' songs are the records of miracles and healings before the beautiful image of Our Lady. Some of the works describe the image. One remarks that it was "tall and stately with a crown upon its head." Another mentions its "golden radiance." From this we may conclude the possibility that the statue may have been gilded.

For nearly three hundred years the miraculous image of Our Lady of Penrhys reigned over her Welsh children in peace and love.

Sadly, in the mid-sixteenth century, the schism of Henry VIII led to a hatred of the church and all things Catholic, and Catholic customs and beliefs were attacked and punished. A campaign of hatred and destruction of shrines was begun, and devotion to Our Lady was attacked as superstition. Hugh Lattimer, the bishop of Worcester, brought Penrhys to the attention of Thomas Cromwell, the vicar-general of the king, in a letter written in 1538, suggesting that the shrine be destroyed. Cromwell acted speedily; the shrine was destroyed in September, and the wondrous statue was taken to London and burned. The farmland at Penrhys was taken away from the monks and given to a nephew of Cromwell.

In spite of the destruction of the shrine and its beautiful image of Our Lady, the sturdy Welsh Catholics kept the faith, and through the years, some continued to visit the now desolate site to offer their prayers and devotion to the Blessed Mother of God, pleading that one day she would return to her children.

Gradually, through the providence of God, the ancient devotion to his Mother began to be rekindled in the hearts of the faithful of South Wales.

At first, interest in Penrhys centered on its historical and archeological aspects. Toward the end of the nineteenth century, the thought of reviving the ancient pilgrimage began to be discussed, and a small trickle of pilgrims began to visit the site. They prayed the rosary, visited the well, and went to a new church nearby for Benediction. Excavations in 1912 gave a good idea of the original size and exact location of the shrine, and unearthed artifacts provided other clues. A convert to the faith generously contributed to the building of a memorial church dedicated to Our Lady of Penrhys at Ferndale. She obtained for the new church a beautiful statue carved from oak and standing in a richly carved tree trunk. The statue, a work of art, was made from the descriptions of the original as found in the writings of the Welsh poets. In 1936, the building containing the holy well was restored. In 1939, the site of the original shrine was purchased by another generous benefactor and given to the archdiocese of Cardiff. Although little development could be done during the dark days of World War II, the children evacuated from the major cities of England who were sent for safety into the Welsh valleys discovered Penrhys as a place of peace and a place to pray for the war-torn world. On their return home, they remembered the peace of Penrhys, and many returned as pilgrims in subsequent years.

The Most Reverend Michael McGrath, archbishop of Cardiff from 1940 to 1961, had a tender love for Our Lady and earnestly wished to bring her devotion back to his archdiocese. He encouraged devotion to Our Lady of Penrhys; and, with the assistance of the Union of Catholic Mothers and the Legion of Mary, he erected a beautiful new image on the site of the original altar of the chapel. Carved from Portland stone, the image is on a pedestal, making its overall height nearly seventeen feet. The descriptions of the original statue found in medieval literature were studied, and the new statue was designed to resemble it as closely as possible. The statue was unveiled by a Cistercian abbot, Dom Malachy Brasil, and blessed by Archbishop McGrath on July 2, 1953.

Today, the magnificent stone image of Our Lady of Penrhys stands as a symbol of the past glories and traditions of her Welsh children, as well as a sign of present-day devotion and a challenge of hope for the future.

We have recently celebrated the fiftieth anniversary of the unveiling of the statue of Our Lady of Penrhys. While devotion and pilgrimages continue, it is a far different world for which we pray. Today we face a crisis in faith, a crisis in vocations, and a crisis in human nature itself. We earnestly beseech the Mother of God for a renewal of faith and devotion especially among our young people; for vocations to the priesthood and religious life; and for an appreciation of all things spiritual as an antidote to the materialism and paganism of our age. O clement, O loving, O sweet Virgin Mary!

—Canon Paul Chidgey

Canon Chidgey is pastor of Ross-on-Wye in Herefordshire, England, which, is part of the archdiocese of Cardiff, Wales.

Mother of Wisdom

Mary, Seat of Wisdom, Sedes Sapientiae
University of St. Thomas, Houston, Texas

Wisdom and knowledge are often associated, and this title of Mary is a favorite of students throughout the world. She is frequently invoked as "help of students."

What I see in the image of Mary is Mary with her hands open, asking us to come to her, to place our needs in her hands—she is our wise and loving mother.

—Hazel Alphonse

Hazel Alphonse is a graduate of the University of St. Thomas. She lives in Castries, St. Lucia.

To read more about Mary, Seat of Wisdom, please visit the special section "Other Faces of Mary" on the author's website: www.annball.com.

Santa María la Real de Nájera
La Virgen de las Cuevas
Nájera, Spain

Santa María la Real is a recurring theme along the road of pilgrimage to the great shrine of Santiago de Compostela in the northern part of Spain. Known as El Camino, the road leads to the city of Santiago de Compostela, where the ancient shrine of St. James has attracted pilgrims for centuries. As pilgrims travel, they frequently encounter images of this Virgin of the Caves along the way in small wayside shrines on buildings, in shop windows, or in the fields. It is as if she is accompanying the travelers with constant reminders of her queenly and motherly presence.

Even a child's jump-rope song celebrates this Virgin of the Caves (*La Virgen de las Cuevas*), asking her protection and blessing on the crops:

> *Que llueva, que llueva*
> *la virgen de las cuevas*
> *los pajaritos cantan*
> *las nubes se levantan*
> *que sí, que no*
> *que caiga un chaparrón*
> *que se mojen los campos*
> *y mi Papi no*

> Let it rain, let it rain
> oh Virgin of the caves
> the birds are singing
> the clouds are lifting
> oh yes, oh no
> let the rain pour down
> let the fields get wet
> but my daddy, no!

Along the pilgrimage route, pilgrims pass the Monastery of Santa María la Real, at Nájera. Here, in restored splendor, the little queen of the caves reigns.

Nájera has been inhabited since prehistoric times and was once one of the greatest of the kingdoms of northern Spain.

Tradition tells that King García of Nájera found the image of Santa María la Real in a cave in 1044.

The story begins in the dark days of the Moorish occupation of Spain. The young king was out hunting when he spotted a partridge and loosed his falcon to catch it. Chased by the falcon, the partridge entered a cave, one of the many natural refuges in the area. Following the birds, the young king was surprised to find them resting at peace with one another in front of a lovely image of the Virgin Mary, sculpted in an elegant, nearly Byzantine style. At her feet stood a vase of lilies, whose sweet perfume scented the air; a silent bell rested nearby. The young king fell to his knees, taking the discovery as the sign of a celestial promise of aid in the soon to be fought battles of the reconquest.

The following year, King García successfully retook Calahorra for the Christians, using the spoils of battle to build a magnificent church with the cave as its center, and a monastery. He took the *terraza,* the vase of lilies, as the emblem for a new order of knights he established in the Virgin's honor. Every Saturday, the king brought his court to worship before his heavenly helper at her altar in the cave.

The statue of Mary is presented enthroned as queen and mother, holding a grown Child Jesus seated on her knee. Her left hand curves protectively about her son, drawing him close to her. The statue is sculpted in three-quarter round of wood and polychrome. Its fine details were restored in 1948. In her right hand, the Virgin holds a queenly scepter; the Child has his right hand raised in blessing.

For centuries, the image of Santa María la Real was venerated in the cave, although she has now been moved and presides over the main altarpiece of the church. True to his wish, the king and his wife, Queen Estefania, were buried in niches carved in the sides of the cave. Their remains were moved during a recent restoration. Another image now stands in the original place of the Virgin in the cave. Carved in the late-thirteenth or early-fourteenth century, this statue originally stood in the Royal Alcazar.

The image, crafted in the period of transition from Romanesque to Gothic style, was restored in 1998.

King García's original church and monastery were staffed with monks of San Isidro, who practiced the Visigoth liturgy. Later the property was turned over to the Benedictines of Cluny. Through the centuries, a number of members of the royal families who ruled this part of Spain were buried here. The royal pantheon is the last resting place of the majority of the royalty of Nájera-Pamplona of the tenth through the twelfth centuries. The great St. Francis of Assisi passed through on pilgrimage in the thirteenth century, and in the sixteenth century, St. Ignatius Loyola lived here for four years in service to the Duke of Navarre, until he was wounded at Pamplona. A number of kings visited to pay their respects to Santa María. As the years passed, the little queen greeted all, pilgrim and king alike, with her gentle gaze of love and interest.

In the early days of the nineteenth century, during the Peninsular War against Napoleon, both the city and the monastery suffered greatly at the hands of the French and guerrillas. Then, for nearly a century of political upheaval, the church and monastery were pillaged and almost ruined. The religious were expelled and the property confiscated. Many beautiful statues were smashed, silver and other valuable items were stolen, and even wooden beams and flooring were removed, causing some parts of the structure to collapse. The buildings were profaned, used as a warehouse, a school, a dancehall, and a military barracks. At last, at the end of the century, the church was returned and began to be used as a parish church again. In 1889, Constantino Garran, an illustrious son of Nájera, recognized the true wealth of the ruins and through his efforts the property was declared a National Monument of Historic and Artistic Interest. In 1895, Franciscan monks came to begin the long work of restoration, which remains an ongoing process even today.

Now, once again, faithful pilgrims to Compostela stop at Nájera to visit the little Queen of the Caves in her sanctuary, adding their voices to the infinite number of those who have evoked her over the centuries in humble, suppliant prayer:

"Hail, Queen and Mother, our life, sweetness and hope. Turn your gaze on us, O merciful sweet Virgin Mary."

My friend Pat and I walked out from the small tree-covered hill and suddenly stepped into a landscape of lined crops and dust fields. Next to a busy highway to our right, I eagerly identified what had to be the famous chapel at Eunate, whose Basque name means "the Hundred Doorways." Described by guidebooks as "one of the jewels" of the pilgrimage route to Santiago de Compostela, the chapel actually required a four- to five-kilometer walking detour off the main route on the Camino de Santiago. Looking back on that morning I remain grateful that the decision whether or not to detour came on the second day of our pilgrimage walk from Pamplona. If we had to make the same decision a week later, I know I would have ignored the guidebooks and obsessed solely about the extra number of kilometers that it would add to our walking day! From the woman living next door to the church, its unofficial caretaker, I learned that the origins of the small octagonal church are obscure. Its unusual shape suggests a link with the Knights Templar, whose churches often resembled the octagonal structure of the Church of the Holy Sepulcher in Jerusalem. Graves marked with scallop shells (the sign of the pilgrims) have been discovered between the church and its surrounding arched cloister, suggesting that Eunate was once a major funerary chapel for pilgrims who died along the Camino de Santiago. I was immediately drawn to the chapel's simple and spartan interior. Floor to ceiling pillar buttresses stretched upward, as if reaching for heaven, and small marble windows let in only a gentle, soft light, making it breathtakingly serene. Only one image stood in the entire church, a mid-size statue of Mary that, I learned (several walking days later) in Nájera, was known as Santa María la Real. She was, indeed, royally dressed, with a gold dress and a gold crown on both hers and Jesus' heads. Perhaps it was the way her left arm lovingly encircled the Child on her lap. But there was something completely disarming in this Mary's smile that instantly won me over. Without words, with only a slight but captivating smile, she told me how much she loved her son. She might be the queen of heaven, but clearly, Santa María la Real was a mother first.

—María Ruiz Scaperlandia

Photo by Vincent Vitale

María Ruiz Scaperlandia is a Catholic author living in Oklahoma with her husband, Michael, and their four children.

Mary, Our Helper

Madonna at Ladyewell
Fernyhalgh, England

The face of the Madonna at Ladyewell is more a feeling than an image. To be sure, the shrine has its statue of Our Lady, a beautiful gift of the Sisters of the Holy Child Jesus in 1935. No apparitions of the Virgin occurred here. Although miraculous favors and cures have been claimed, they are not the focus of this hallowed place. A number of relics of England's martyrs are on display in the shrine today, but there is no written record that proves that any of them were here during their lifetime. Yet the heroism and the grace of their offering can almost be touched at this ancient and sacred shrine, hallowed by centuries of prayer and devotion to the Mother of God. Here at Our Lady's well, the greatest cure is the mending of human brokenness.

Fernyhalgh (pronounced Ferny-uff) is an Anglo-Saxon name meaning "ancient shrine." There was probably a pagan shrine here that was Christianized in the seventh century after the king of Northumbria was baptized. In its earliest Christian days it probably served as an Anglo-Saxon baptistry.

Tucked away in a sleepy and remote corner of Lancashire, once noted as the most Catholic region of England, the shrine annually attracts a steady stream of pilgrims. It is a place of prayer and a shrine of thanksgiving.

In common with many shrines worldwide, Ladyewell has a romantic story to explain its history. Around 1100, an Irish merchant, Fergus Maguire, was returning home on a heavily laden galley on the Irish sea, when a storm threatened to sink the ship. The crew had resigned themselves to death when Fergus, the younger son of a chief of Fermanagh and owner of the galley, fell on his knees and begged God to aid him. He promised that if he was saved, he would perform some pious action. The ship rode out the storm, and, once on land, the exhausted merchant slept. In his dreams, he heard the heavenly voice of Our Lady telling him to go to Fernyhalgh and to build her a chapel in the place where he would find an apple tree bearing fruit with no core.

The ship had made port at what is now Liverpool. True to his vow, Fergus began to hunt for Fernyhalgh, but his inquiries came to naught. No one had ever heard of the place. Leaving his galley in competent hands, he sought far and wide for the place he had been directed to find by the heavenly voice.

At last one evening he stopped at a farmhouse, where the lady of the house was standing by the gate as if waiting for someone.

She invited him in to rest, telling him she would remain watching for her servant who had taken the cows to pasture and was late in returning. Some time later, he was aroused by the sound of voices. As the lady scolded her servant, the girl justified her lateness, explaining that one of the cows had wandered off. "I found her at Fernyhalgh." As proof of where she had been, the girl showed the branch of an apple tree which she said she had broken from the tree by the well there. Excited to hear mention of the place he had sought so long, Fergus examined the fruit on the branch and discovered that, just as he had been told, it had no core.

The following day, he set off with the maid as guide; and when they reached the well, Fergus assured himself that it was the right place and said a prayer of thanksgiving.

Fergus found a stone near the well that had a tracery in the shape of mother and child, and realized that Our Lady had once been honored here. He kept his promise and built a chapel so that she could be honored at the sacred place once more.

Although it is certain that a chapel had existed at Ladyewell for centuries, the earliest documentary evidence is a license in the archives of the York diocese which is dated in the mid-fourteenth century.

In 1547, the first year of the reign of Edward VI, an act of parliament assigned to the Crown all chantries and free chapels. The chapel at Ladyewell was destroyed; its revenues, furniture, and bell were confiscated. Today, archaeologists believe that the site of this chapel, probably the one built by Fergus Maguire, was in the field opposite the well.

Even after the destruction of the chapel, the devotion of the Catholics remained; and they continued to come to Ladyewell to pray and give homage to the Mother of God. In the severest times of the persecutions, the remoteness of the area must have attracted many as a comparatively safe place to seek solace.

When James II came to the throne in 1685, the persecutions abated somewhat, and Ladyewell House was built to serve as a center for Mass.

In outward appearance, the house was identical to many other large dwellings of the area. The ground floor was used as a priest's residence and the upper floor as a chapel. Delighted to be able to worship in a church again, Catholics for miles around flocked to the house. In 1687, 1,099 people were confirmed there. Although the number seems incredible, it must be remembered that there had not been a bishop in the country for thirty years. Sadly, the hopes raised by the accession of a Catholic king were soon dashed when he fled the country and the persecutions began again. Although the house was plundered and stripped of anything moveable, it was not destroyed. Priests continued to live there, sometimes openly and sometimes clandestinely.

In 1795, the present St. Mary's Church was built. Though Catholic emancipation had not yet been officially passed, there was comparative freedom to practice the faith, and churches were once again being built.

The English hierarchy was restored in 1850. With the opening of St. Mary's, the chapel at Ladyewell House was no longer used, but pilgrims still came to the Lady Well to pray.

In 1905, the Sisters of the Holy Child Jesus came at the request of the archbishop of Liverpool, and the Blessed Sacrament was brought back to Ladyewell House. The well was renovated, and paving stones were laid which enabled pilgrims to go safely down to the well. In 1935, a statue of Our Lady and the Child Jesus was placed in an arch near the well.

The sisters remained at Ladyewell until 1985. During the eighty years of their presence, they preserved the sacred atmosphere and kept alive the spirit of Ladyewell.

In 1987, a priest chaplain and a laywoman were appointed custodians of the ancient shrine with a directive to welcome and meet the needs of the pilgrims. Improvements and modern conveniences have been added to the shrine, but they have not been allowed to detract from its sacred space.

Today, just as she has done for centuries past, Our Lady of the Well beckons the weary pilgrim to come and pray, to seek solace and comfort, and to leave refreshed.

If you are a first-time visitor on your own, you won't find Ladyewell easily. It lies deep in the Lancashire countryside, in a tiny village that doesn't appear on any map. You reach it by a succession of quiet roads, at the end of a long, winding track where oncoming cars have to maneuver to pass each other.

After days of rain I arrived on a bright, sunlit morning. My wife had died two months before, and I hoped to find the comfort that had so far eluded me. Our Lady did not disappoint me. After drinking the water and praying at the well, my heart at last began to lift.

The sadness, the regrets, the guilt for past unkindness . . . they didn't go away, but they somehow fell into place, and I was able to measure them against the joy that we shared in our children and grandchildren, the many good times we enjoyed, and, above all, our special closeness during Pat's last illness.

Especially moving was Benediction in the chapel of Ladyewell House, given by the shrine's chaplain, Canon Benedict Ruscillo, who was about to celebrate the sixtieth anniversary of his ordination. At the age of 68 I looked with awe at a priest who had been ordained when I was a child in primary school.

Benediction . . . remember that? Somewhat to my surprise I found that I could sing O Salutaris Hostia *and* Tantum Ergo *without hesitating over a word—well, almost. We had a decade of the rosary and a number of traditional prayers, including the prayer to St. Michael, which, in preconciliar days, used to be offered for Russia at the end of every Low Mass.*

With its traditional piety and long history, Ladyewell symbolizes for me a Catholicism rooted in the past—in the devotion of the medieval pilgrims and the sacrifices of penal days. It would, I am sure, move any Catholic to pray before an altar where Mass had been celebrated by priests who died for the faith—including two canonized martyrs, St.

Edmund Campion and St. Edmund Arrowsmith. The altar, now in Ladyewell House, was commissioned by a Lancashire family and designed to look like a cupboard when not in use.

During the days of persecution it was in Lancashire, above all, that Catholics held on to the faith. "Catholic Lancashire" is a description still sometimes used—especially by those of us who happen to be Lancastrians! Many of those brave folk crossed the fields to Ladyewell to pray to Our Lady, and although there is no direct evidence that any of the martyrs came to the shrine, they may well have done so. One of the canonized martyrs, St. John Southworth, was born and raised at Samlesbury, just a few miles away. St. John Wall was also born in Lancashire.

Remote in its location and with no recorded appearance of the Blessed Virgin, Ladyewell is far less well-known than the great English shrine at Walsingham, two hundred miles away. Nevertheless, it attracts a steady stream of pilgrims each year. As I drove away, feeling so much happier than when I arrived, I realized that for me this quiet place also symbolized something else: the hidden, undramatic spirit in which Our Lady spent so much of her life at Nazareth.

—Leo Knowles

Leo Knowles is a Catholic author who lives in England. He is known to the American public through numerous articles in the Catholic press and two current books as well as through his previous books on the lives of the saints.

Our Lady of Montligeon
Montligeon, France

The holy souls cannot help themselves. Their greatest pain is the loss of the sight of God. Only we can get them out. And in return, the holy souls pray and intercede for us all the days of our lives until we are safely home in Heaven. They become our friends forever! What a gift! Our Lady of Montligeon is the Mother of the Souls in Purgatory. She intercedes for the holy souls to release them from Purgatory. Our Lord never says no to His Mother! Our Lady of Montligeon, pray for our Dead!

—Susan Tassone

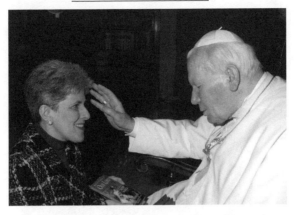

Susan Tassone is the author of *The Stations of the Cross for the Holy Souls in Purgatory.*

To read more about Our Lady of Montligeon please visit the special section "Other Faces of Mary" on the author's website: www.annball.com.

Virgin with Three Hands
The Image of the Most Holy Theotokos
the Troyeruchitsa (Trojerucica)
Greece

The first anathema of St. Cyril, archbishop of Alexandria, who presided at the ecumenical council of Ephesus in 431, states: "If anyone should not confess that Emmanuel is truly God and that in consequence, the Holy Virgin is *theotokos*—for she brought forth according to the flesh the Word of God made flesh—let him be anathema."

Since that time, the Greek word *theotokos,* or God bearer, has been the lynchpin of Mariology. The great Cardinal Newman wrote of the word that it "carries with it no admixture of rhetoric, no taint of extravagant affection. . . . It intends to express that God is her Son, as truly as any one of us is the son of his own mother."

The Greek word *eikon,* or icon, simply means an image, but the term has become characteristic of the stylized painted wooden panels that are the characteristic sacred images of the Christian East. A long dispute arose within the Byzantine Empire during the middle of the sixth century over the veneration of icons. The iconoclasts ("breakers of images") used the biblical prohibition of graven images in their argument to ban the veneration of icons and other religious images. In the middle of the seventh century, the Byzantine Empress Theodora called for the restoration of the holy icons. During this long controversy, politics, especially those of church and state, were involved, but there were also serious theological issues as well. A number of these issues were resolved during the Second Council of Nicea in 787. The most distinguished defender of the icons was St. John of Damascus (ca. 675–ca. 749).

The saint, known as John Damascene, is a Doctor of the Church and the last of the Greek Fathers. He is venerated by the Orthodox in both the Eastern and Western Churches. Born in Damascus, Syria, he succeeded his father as an advisor to the caliph. In 719, he was compelled to resign his post because of his Christian faith. He entered a monastery near Jerusalem, where he concentrated on prayer and writing. He authored over 150 works, as well as many poems. His writings include his famous defenses of the veneration of icons against the iconoclastic emperor Leo the Isaurian.

Although much of his work remains, it is surprising how little is known of his life. The biography of him written by John of Jerusalem about two hundred years after his death is a mix of facts and legends which are difficult to sort out. One legend, which is apocryphal but nonetheless charming, concerns the Trojerucica, an icon of the Virgin with three hands.

The legend tells that Leo the Isaurian caused a forged letter, treasonous and purportedly written by the saint, to be sent to the sultan. In retaliation, the angry sultan ordered the guilty hand of the traitor to be cut off. John knelt before the Virgin's image, praying in faithful entreaty that his hand might be restored to him. He fell asleep and woke with his hand as before. Convinced by the miracle that he was under the special protection of the Theotokos, he determined to devote himself entirely to a life of prayer and retired to the monastery of St. Sabas. In gratitude to the Mother of God, he ordered that a representation of his hand be made in silver; he fastened it to the icon before which the miracle was performed and presented the icon to the monastery. (Some sources claim that John simply drew or painted the third hand on the icon.) This icon became known as "Three handed."

The icon was later given as a blessing to St. Sabbas, the archbishop of Serbia (d. 1237), and it was venerated particularly in Skopje, the capital of the Serbian empire. When the Turks invaded Serbia, the precious icon was given into the custody of the Holy Mount Athos Monastery of Hilandar (Serbian). The decision to give it to the monastery on Mount Athos is attributed to the miraculous intervention of God's providence.

The Trojerucica is a large processional icon, covered by silver and gold frames and *ex votos* which conceal a Virgin and Child of the Hodeghetria type.

In 1661, a copy of the wonder-working icon was brought to Moscow and is now located there in the Holy Dormition Temple of the Bulgarian Metochion. Copies of the icon became widely distributed throughout Russia, and later throughout the world.

The third hand of the Theotokos on this icon reminds us that Our Lady is always willing to aid those who appeal to her in faith.

> *I was inspired to paint the Virgin of Three Hands after reading the legend of St. John Damascene. Although some believe that the hand was put on the icon to represent the hand of God, I was impressed by the idea of such faith. The lovely faces of Mary and Jesus in this particular icon seemed very consoling. I was drawn to the idea and also to the physical visual image.*
>
> —Mary Talamini

Mary Talamini is an artist in Houston, Texas. She painted the copy of the icon of the Virgin with Three Hands shown on p. 115.

"Rejoice, blesssed Gate-keeper, who openest to the faithful the doors of paradise."

Akathist refrain

Vailankanni Arokia Matha
Our Lady of Health
Vailankanni, India

The millions who visit the shrine seem borne on a wave of love; they have come to their mother, who heals them of their wounds, physical and spiritual. What moves me and, I suspect, most of the other pilgrims is the maternal presence of Mary that transcends buildings and crowds and even the miraculous spring. This is the presence that draws us there, softening our hearts, purifying our souls and replacing nameless loneliness with unutterable love.

—Roy Abraham Varghese

Roy Abraham Varghese is author/editor of eight books on the interaction of science, philosophy, and theology. He resides in Dallas, Texas.

For the history of the image of Vailankanni Arokia Matha please visit the special section "Other Faces of Mary" on the author's website: www.annball.com.

Our Lady of Tra Kieu
Tra Kieu, Vietnam

The first Catholic missionaries entered Indochina (Vietnam) in 1533. A scant hundred years later, there were over one hundred thousand Catholics in the area. Severe persecutions broke out in 1698, and waves of persecution have covered the Vietnamese Catholic Church since that time. Through the centuries, the soil of Vietnam has been liberally watered with the blood of Christian martyrs. Even today, especially in the north, the oppressive economic and political situation of the country stifles the freedom of the church. Nonetheless, the blood of her martyrs has been the seed of a lively and enduring faith in Vietnam.

Little known in the free world, two apparitions of Mary occurred in Vietnam, both in the midst of persecution. Different from many of the other major apparitions of the Virgin, in Vietnam the appearances of Our Lady did not convey messages of repentance or require anything of her people. Instead, at La Vang and Tra Kieu, she appeared as a powerful harbinger of mercy, a protective mother full of love for her suffering children.

In his encyclical *Dives in misericordia,* Pope John Paul II describes Mary as the "Mother of Mercy," who has "the deepest knowledge of God's mercy. She knows its price, she knows how great it is." It is this Mother of Mercy who is so loved by Vietnamese Catholics.

At the end of the seventeenth century, the persecution in central Vietnam was so severe that many Catholics fled to a mountainous region near Lavang. Here, the Queen of Heaven appeared to her persecuted children, speaking to them in the loving tones of a mother, comforting them and teaching them how to make medicines from the plants in the area. She promised her protection to those who would come there to pray. Eventually a beautiful shrine was built, and the people came in procession to worship until the shrine was destroyed during the Vietnam war. The devotion of the people remained strong, and even today Catholics go to the site for prayerful reflection and, when permitted by the government, on pilgrimage.

Closer to our own times, Our Lady appeared at Tra Kieu to defend a band of Catholics who were fighting for their lives in the persecution of 1885. Ironically, just as happened at Peking a scant fifteen years later, it was only through the testimony of the pagans, or unbelievers, that the Virgin's protection was brought to light. The Christians themselves saw nothing.

In 1885, another wave of persecution rolled over the Vietnamese church. A pro-royal movement called "Can Vuong" was initiated by the young emperor Ham Nghi to fight against French colonial power. Ham Nghi, who ascended the throne in 1884, was arrested by the French in 1888 and exiled to Algeria. While he reigned, however, the blood of Catholics flowed freely. He wanted to eradicate the French presence in the country and destroy the "false religion." Many members of another movement called "Van Than" (literati) joined with the Can Vuong in the persecution.

Tra Kieu, a small village of some nine hundred inhabitants, in the province of Quang Nam, south of Hue, had a parish church. On September 1, 1885, the parish along with its people and their pastor, Father Jean Bruyère, was surrounded by the Can Vuong. The Catholics were desperate, outnumbered three to one, and they had very few weapons. Father Bruyère urged them to place their confidence in Mary. A picture of the Virgin was placed on a table in the church, surrounded with candles. Father Bruyère explained that the fighting against the raiders was in self-defense, and the Catholics nominated the Holy Mother as their supreme commander. As the young men went out to fight, the old people, women, and children prayed in front of the image, constantly saying the rosary and pleading for the Virgin's help.

Despite the overwhelming odds, the attacking force was held at bay for several days. Finally, the Can Vuong brought in cannons and began shooting at the church. They constantly missed their mark. One of the mandarins later said that he had seen a beautiful woman dressed in white standing on top of the church, and that although he took aim at her he was never able to hit her. Others of the attackers confirmed the presence of the lady.

At last, on September 21, the Can Vuong decided on a final assault on the parish church. They brought elephants to assist in the attack, which terrified the Catholics, but the sturdy defenders frightened the beasts away with flaming torches.

The Catholics could stand no more, and the defenders turned to the attack, led by the able missionary Father Bruyère. Even the women carried sabers and followed the men into the fray. As they went forward, the Catholics chanted the names Jesus and Mary continuously.

The valiant priest diverted the attention of the Can Vuong, and the villagers were able to creep up from behind to rout the enemy. The leader of the Can Vuong was decapitated, and most of the rest threw down their weapons and fled. A number of the defeated Can Vuong testified that large groups of children dressed in white and red had come down from the bamboo plants and marched in front of the attacking Catholics. Hearing the stories of the lady on the church and of the children, none of whom were seen by the Catholics, they naturally attributed their improbable victory to the protection of the Queen of Heaven. That night, the jubilant Catholics gathered around the image of the Holy Mother, thanking her and blessing her for saving them.

In 1898 a chapel was built in Tra Kieu, dedicated to Mary, Help of Christians, and in 1959 and 1971 pilgrimages with a large number of participants were organized to this Marian sanctuary.

Today, a Catholic village still stands in the area of Tra Kieu. The church was built on the grounds of the former Cham capital, one of the ancient kingdoms of the area. A number of Cham relics are preserved in the church.

Wearing yellow scarves to solemnize the celebration, Catholics pilgrims come to Our Lady's shrine at Tra Kieu annually on May 31.

Our Lady of Vocations Worldwide

Throughout the history of the church, Our Lady has been the inspiration of thousands of dedicated religious men and women who have devoted their lives to the service of God. Religious orders and congregations have been founded in her honor. Each order of religious generally has a particular favorite among the thousands of images of Mary. Although many are familiar with the images of Our Lady of Mt. Carmel and Our Lady of Sorrows, so revered by the Carmelites and the Servites, others have portrayed her with the symbols or attributes of their own group or with members of their order. A few of these faces of Mary are shown here.

Mother of Vocations

This title comes from the Rogationists, who have a worldwide mission to work for an increase in vocations. An Italian priest, St. Hannibal Mary Di Francia, became the apostle of the gospel command "Pray the Lord of the harvest to send laborers into his harvest." He founded two congregations, the Rogationists of the Sacred Heart of Jesus and the Daughters of Divine Zeal, and entrusted their work to the "Queen and Mother of the Evangelical Rogation." There are a number of images of Mary as Mother of Vocations. One of them, painted by an Italian artist around 1930, shows Mary with her arms outstretched to six young men, inviting them to the religious life.

Our Lady of the Blessed Sacrament

St. Peter Julian Eymard, the great apostle of the Eucharist, placed his religious order, the Congregation of the Blessed Sacrament, under the guidance and protection of Our Lady of the Blessed Sacrament. The Virgin and her Divine Son are portrayed with the chalice and host in a number of artistic representations. One is a beautiful stained glass window at the General House in Rome, Italy.

Our Lady of the Passion

St. Paul of the Cross, founder of the Passionist order, had a vision of Our Lady which, years later, he described to a young woman he was directing. The saint had seen a vision of Mary with the sign of the passion on her breast, a heart on which was a white cross such as Passionists wear today. Paul described the Virgin as "most beautiful." In the vision, she spoke to him, saying, "Son, you see how I am clothed in mourning. This is for the most sorrowful passion of my beloved Son, Jesus. You must be clothed in the same way, and you are to found a congregation which will be dressed this way to mourn continuously for the passion and death of my dear Son." One lovely painting of the Virgin with the Passionist symbol also includes a small angel holding the rule book of the congregation.

Our Lady of the Christian Brothers

The title Our Lady of the Star, Queen and Mother of the Christian Schools, is one that is dear to the de la Salle Brothers of the Christian Schools. One medieval sanctuary in her honor was rebuilt after the French revolution by the Brothers of the Christian Schools of Mercy, a diocesan community that followed the rule of de la Salle and which later was incorporated into the Lasallian Institute. In an artistic representation, possibly created in the 1950s and known as Our lady of the Christian Brothers, Mary is shown with a star as her halo, echoing the devotion to Our Lady of the Star. She is shown with a brother in the habit of the institute and with a student as representative of the teaching mission of the brothers.

The Legion of Mary

One picture of the Virgin depicts the objectives of the Legion of Mary, an international lay organization begun in Ireland. Mary is shown crushing the serpent (Satan). Soldiers symbolize the legion's armies. Their banner, with the Latin words *"Legio Maria,"* is displayed proudly as is their standard signifying the predominance of the Holy Spirit guiding the members in bringing the knowledge of Christ into the world.

Our Lady of the Jesuits

A large mural over the main altar of St. Charles Borromeo Church at the St. Francis Mission in South Dakota was painted by one of the former students of the school who was a native American member of the Sicangu Lakota Oyate (Burnt Thigh Nation). The mural depicts Our Lady with a number of the Jesuit saints and martyrs.

Our Lady of the Most Holy Trinity

Our Lady is the guiding light for the members of the Society of Our Lady of the Most Holy Trinity (S.O.L.T.), a relatively new group in the church. Based on the concept of following Jesus Christ after the example of Mary in relationship with the Trinity, the group is a religious society with ecclesial teams of priests, religious, and laity. Established in New Mexico in 1958, the society received its decree of canonical approval in 1994. Blessed with rapid growth in membership, the society has spread throughout the world. The image of Our Lady of the Most Holy Trinity has a depiction of the trinity on her breast.

A multitude of glorious images of Our Lady call us to remember that in all states of life, religious or lay, we are called to the vocation of sanctity. She invites us with welcoming hands to accompany her in true adoration of the triune God.

Our Lady of the Trinity . . . how much she has taught me. She has taught me about the nature of the universe. All of creation is made in the image, not of a solitary God (as St.

Hillary of Poitiers says), but in the image of the Most Holy Trinity. All of creation longs for union in Christ. Mary of the Trinity has taught me of the church. The church is a family that reflects also the Most Holy Trinity. He is the primordial Family. He is God, who from all eternity has lived in loving relationship, the Father loving the Son and the Holy Spirit, the Son loving the Father and the Holy Spirit, the Holy Spirit being the living breath of love between the Father and the Holy Spirit. The church is a hurricane of love that images the Trinity.

Mary of the Trinity has also taught me of myself. I too am made in the image of the Triune God, I too, intrinsically, necessarily, exist to love. I too, by my very nature which images the Trinity, am made to give myself away in love for the rest of eternity. I too must give myself away in love as the Father gives himself to the Son, and give myself to the communion of saints and sinners, just as Jesus does for all time and eternity.

—Father Anthony Anderson

Rev. Anthony "Tony" Anderson is a priest of the Society of Our Lady of the Holy Trinity, currently serving in Mexico.

Ina Poon Bato
Zambales, Philippines

The legend of Ina Poon Bato tells that over four hundred years ago an Aeta chieftain was resting from an unsuccessful hunt when he heard a woman's voice calling to him, asking to be taken home.

Looking around, he found an image of a beautiful woman carved in wood. When he returned home and gave the statue to his wife, she angrily threw it into the fire, scolding him for his failure to bring food for his children. The fire flared up, and the entire house burned; but the image was unharmed. Djadig, the chieftain, announced the miracle to his tribe, who henceforth began to venerate the image.

The Aetas are an indigenous race of short, dark-skinned people who probably first appeared in the Philippines about thirty thousand years ago and who may have crossed a land bridge that once connected the islands to mainland Asia. A people who live close to nature, they have been staunch allies of the United States through the years by rescuing downed pilots during World War II and by helping to train American soldiers in jungle survival.

In the first days of the seventeenth century, when the Augustinian Recollects (*Recoletos*) arrived in Zambales, they heard stories of the miraculous lady of the Aetas. Thinking this was part of a primitive cult, the priests wanted to see the image. On seeing it, they were amazed that the image was of the Blessed Mother, and they wondered how she could have arrived before them, paving the way for their coming. The image was taken to their church, where it remained until it was moved to the church of the Dominican missionaries in 1712. In 1897, the image was moved to a chapel at the foothills of Mount Pinatubo.

In 1976, a lovely copy of Ina Poon Bato was made by the sculptor Maximo Vicente at the request of the Columban Fathers, and in the 1980s it became the rallying symbol for the Holy Rosary Crusade for World Peace.

In 1991, one of the most moving images of the eruption of Mount Pinatubo showed pictures of Ina buried in the mudflow in the grotto at Botolan, Zambales. At this time, Pope John Paul II received a copy of the statue and led prayers for the volcano's victims. Her devotees in Botolan prayed the rosary by the hour, pleading for divine aid and venerating the image and its two replicas. They credited Ina Poon Bato with saving the town from destruction by the volcano, although the town's inhabitants were later resettled because Mount Pinatubo's crater lake had been breached.

On January 23 and 24 there is an annual fiesta in honor of Ina Poon Bato which is the biggest fiesta of the province. Over one hundred thousand people attend. Since the original town was buried after the eruption of Mount Pinatubo, the celebration is now held in the resettlement area of Danag Bunga, where many of the original residents of Poon Bato now reside.

Although the Philippines have been blessed with a number of beautiful and interesting images of Our Lady, none is more loved and venerated by her people than Ina Poon Bato, the oldest image in the islands.

> *Our community is constantly bombarded by threats and danger posed by Muslim extremists and rebels. But, with our fervent devotion to Our Lady as Ina Poon Bato, to whom we always run for refuge and safety, we have always been spared from any evils and peril. This we attribute through the most powerful intercession of Ina Poon Bato, who always watches over us.*
>
> —Sr. Andrea Margarita

Sister Andrea is a member of the Franciscan Sisters of Manila, stationed in La Huerta, Philippines.

The Virgin Who Unties Knots
Germany—Argentina—United States

An ancient German devotion to Mary under an unusual title has taken Argentina by storm in recent years, and in 2003 it immigrated to the United States.

The devotion to "La Virgen María Desatadora de Nudos," or the "Virgin as Untier of Knots," became enormously popular a few years ago in Argentina after Argentinean movie stars, boxers, singers, and soccer players began referring to the *Desatanudos* as though it were some kind of talisman or New Age divinity. The Catholic Church in Buenos Aires reacted promptly to this trend of public invocation to clarify the true Marian character of the devotion.

The Virgen María Desatadora de Nudos was brought to Argentina in the early 1980s by Jesuit Father Jorge Bergoglio, who was then rector at the Jesuit University of El Salvador but who went on to become the cardinal archbishop of Buenos Aires. He had found the image at the church of St. Peter am Perlach during a visit to Augsburg, Germany. He was intrigued by the odd name and image of Mary called *Knotenlöserin,* the "One Who Unties Knots."

The seventeenth-century Baroque painting is attributed to the German artist Johann Melchior Georg Schmittner and represents the Virgin with an angel on her left side handing her a white ribbon filled with knots. As the ribbon winds through Mary's hands, it falls to her right side, with the knots untied, into the hands of a second celestial denizen. The dove of the Holy Spirit seems to shower graces on the humbly inclined head of Mary, while a choir of cherubim looks on.

Father Bergoglio was impressed by the powerful message of the Virgin as the one who unties the knots of our lives. He brought several postcards with the image back to Argentina and commissioned the painting of a replica of the image, which remains today in the chapel of the university.

For nearly twenty years, the devotion remained mostly unknown, except among the university's students, professors, and visiting Catholic scholars.

In 1996, three parishioners of San José de Talar, a suburban parish of Buenos Aires, asked Father Rodolfo Arroyo if they could have permission to promote devotion to La Virgen María Desatadora de Nudos. Knowing nothing of the devotion, Father Arroyo approached Cardinal Antonio Quarracino, who in turn referred him to his vicar general and auxiliary, Bishop Bergoglio, who was both surprised and delighted with the idea.

Devotees at the parish decided to build a small chapel for her and hoped to inaugurate it on December 8th of that year. Father Arroyo approved of the project but warned them that there were many obstacles, not the least was the pressing need for financing. The devotees serenely told him that the Virgin herself would untie the knots.

A few days later, the famous Argentinian artist Ana Betta de Berti offered to paint a copy of the image. In less than two weeks, architects, masons, and other parishioners offered their construction expertise, time, and money. By December 8, 1996, the solemnity of the Immaculate Conception, the chapel of La Virgen María Desatadora de Nudos was dedicated.

In 2003, Father Alejandro Russo, general vicar of the archdiocese of Argentina, published a flyer on the history of the image, which is distributed to pilgrims and devotees.

"I immediately started to experience evident changes at the parish. More and more people started to come to the chapel to pray to the Mother of God," Father Arroyo said. On the eighth of each month, the church is packed for Mass. On December 8, 1998, two years after the chapel opened, seventy thousand pilgrims practically besieged the small suburban parish.

Today, the image of the Virgen María Desatadora de Nudos can be found in several other parishes in Argentina. In May of 2003, her image was enthroned at St. Joseph's Church in Del Rio, Texas, the first Virgen María Desatadora de Nudos to be enshrined in the United States.

The theological implication of the *Knotenlöserin* is a very ancient one, going back to St. Irenaeus, a second-century father of the church. In his writings, Irenaeus explains that just as Eve sinned and tied the knots of sin and evil, so Mary, the New Eve, unties these knots.

Mario H. Ibertis Rivera, a married Catholic businessman and father of four from Buenos Aires, did extensive research to find the origin and background of the image. In particular, he wanted to counter the magic and esoteric practices resulting from the lack of information that he saw creeping into the true Marian character of the devotion because of its enormous upsurge in popularity at the end of the 1990s. He conducted his inquiries within the fields of German history, sacred art, the Jesuits, and ancient costumes—research made more difficult because German archives were destroyed during World War II, and the image was little known in her own country.

Eventually, he was able to discover the name of the painter and unearth records showing that the painting was commissioned by Father Hieronymus Ambrosius Langenmantel, a priest and doctor of canon law at St. Peter am Perlach from 1666 to 1709.

The story tells that in 1612 a noble named Wolfgang Langenmantel was on the verge of divorce from his wife, Sophie. He visited with the learned Jesuit Jakob Rem in the city of Ingolstadt for council and prayer, and, in the company of the priest, venerated an image of the Blessed Virgin. Changes in their family life occurred, and the troubles of the marriage were resolved in 1615. Father Hieronymus, the grandson of Wolfgang, donated the painting as a family altar in gratitude to the Virgin for her favors to his family and in commemoration of the turn of the century.

The image of the Virgen María Desatadora de Nudos presents a beautiful symbol of Mary as the one who unties the knots of our lives, in particular those of married life. An old wedding custom in Germany is probably the basis for the ribbon the artist has painted in Mary's hands. At the wedding ceremony, the arms of the bride and groom were tied together with a white ribbon as a symbol of unity. The couple preserved the ribbon as a keepsake. In some families, the couple would tie a knot in the ribbon when they had a problem, and untie it when the problem was solved. A remnant of this custom can be seen today among the Pennsylvania German and Dutch in the United States. In Latin American countries it is a prevalent custom during the wedding ceremony for the bride and groom to be physically joined with a bridal ribbon or lasso to symbolize that the couple is united forever. They see the ribbon in the hands of the Virgin in the painting as a lasso, and the Virgin as the one who will untangle the knots of troubled marriages.

Priests, too, can find a special appeal in this image, if they look on the ribbon in the Virgin's hands as symbolic of the *manutergium*. Formerly, after the bishop had anointed a new priest's hands with chrism during the ordination ceremony, an acolyte would wind the *manutergium,* or ribbon of white linen, around his folded hands. Before the concelebration of the Mass, the new priest's hands were wiped clean with this ribbon. Standing as *regina cleri,* la Virgen María Desatadora de Nudos will also aid the clergy in untying the knots of their lives.

"Mary is the one who unties all kinds of knots from our personal sins, so she can untie the knots in marriage as well," Ibertis Rivera says. "Although ancient, the devotion to La Virgen María Desatadora de Nudos is also contemporary and relevant to today's Catholics." His words find corroboration in the Second Vatican Council's Dogmatic Constitution on the Church: "The knot of Eve's disobedience was untied by Mary's obedience; what Eve bound through her disbelief, Mary loosened by her faith" (*Lumen Gentium,* no. 56).

In a written description of the traditional image, Cardinal Bergoglio highlights the fact that the angel who presents Mary with the knots is looking directly at the Virgin, while the angel who receives the untied ribbon is looking, in a more illuminated area of the painting, directly toward the observer. "In this way," the cardinal explains, "the angel is telling us: 'Look! This is what she can do with the knots of your sins and with the knots in your personal life.'"

Himself a staunch devotee of Mary as Untier of Knots, Mario Ibertis-Rivera wrote a novena and twenty-eight-day devotion in honor of the Virgin and began a prayer group with the hope of spreading the devotion's fraternity worldwide. Rosie and Henry Aguilar, active parishioners of St. Joseph's Catholic Church in Del Rio, Texas, brought the devotion to the United States. With the blessing of Archbishop Patrick Flores of San Antonio, and their parish priest, Father Ramiro Cortez, they spearheaded the campaign to enthrone the image in their parish church. They received two copies of the Desatanudos image from Ibertis-Rivera—a large painting to be enshrined in the church and a smaller one to be used as a pilgrim Virgin.

At the enthronement in May 2003, as part of the ceremony, four special rosaries representing the joyful, sorrowful, glorious, and luminous mysteries were presented to the Virgin by various parish groups and organizations. A prayer group in Del Rio promotes devotion to Our Lady, and the pilgrim Virgin image has begun visiting homes in the city. On the first day of her visit, the prayer group joins in the rosary. She then stays for a week in the home while the family offers daily devotions and gathers items to be given as charity to the poor. The group hopes to eventually be able to construct a special shrine dedicated to the Virgin Who Unties Knots.

My husband, Henry, and I both have devotion to Our Lady, and we believe that Jesus is very pleased when we go to him through her. In this title the Virgin Mary is untying knots, the knots of a matrimonial ribbon, as was the tradition in Germany. The way we got to know about this devotion is through the internet. One time someone asked about "La Virgen Desatanudos." I had never heard about this title, so I searched online and there was a huge website in Spanish telling about the devotion in Argentina. Since my husband and I are bilingual, we decided to look on the English section of the site, and to our surprise the word "worship" was everywhere and not to Our Lord but to Our Lady, which is not correct. When we looked on the Spanish site, the word used was "venerar," which is not "worship" but "venerate," which is correct, and so we felt we should say something to Mr. Ibertis. We wrote him an e-mail and told him about how the word "worship" is not correct for the Virgin Mary but only for God, and he immediately changed the word to "venerate," which in Spanish was no problem; but for some reason his software had translated it to "worship." He then asked Henry and me if we would like to help him in the mis-

sion of spreading the devotion in the United States and Mexico. We prayed about it and we said "yes," and ever since that "yes" to God, we have not stopped. We talked to our parish priest, Father Ramiro, and to Archbishop Flores, and everything has been coming out pretty smooth, just as if Our Lady was untying all the knots in this mission.

We have formed the Virgin Mary Untier of Knots Society, which ministers to the poor and spreads the devotion; and we have plans to build a shrine to the Virgin Mary Untier of Knots. We pray that through this devotion, we all may get closer to God and his church.

—Rosie Aguilar

Rosie and her husband, Henry,
live in Del Rio, Texas.

The Good Shepherdess

Divina Pastora
Siparia, Trinidad, West Indies

At the parish church of Siparia, Trinidad, a dark-skinned Madonna is honored under the title of La Divina Pastora, the Holy Shepherdess. Since the 1880s, she has become a point of crosscultural and interreligious contact, because on Holy Thursday thousands of pilgrims of the Hindu faith also come to honor her. Muslims and Christian groups also hold the Divina Pastora in high reverence.

The image of Divina Pastora is a Spanish baroque bust on wooden struts with joined arms, which, when dressed, gives the impression of a full-figured statue. It is two-and-one-half feet tall and is made of African cedar, covered with a thin layer of gesso which has been smoothed and painted. The face and hands are dark copper, which gives her an Amerindian appearance. She has real, shiny black hair. At one time she wore a beautiful gold crown, but it was stolen in 1974. Today, its replacement is only worn on special feast days. She carries a shepherd's staff in her right hand, and the image is frequently dressed in new clothing by women of the parish.

In 1703, the Blessed Virgin appeared to a venerable Capuchin Monk, Isidore of Seville, in the province of Aragon in Spain. Appearing in the costume of an Andalusian shepherdess, she gave her name as La Divina Pastora and made known her mission to bring people into the sheepfold of her Divine Son. The title became a popular one among the Capuchin Order, and in 1795 Pope Pius VI named La Divina Pastora as patroness of the Capuchin missions and established a special feast in her honor. During the most recent revision of the church calendar, the feast was set for the third Sunday after Easter.

The Capuchins established missions in Venezuela in the early eighteenth century, and by mid-century their work had spread to the island of Trinidad, where they established a number of missions, including one at Siparia, which they dedicated under the title of Divina Pastora. Here they worked among the Amerindians, in particular those of the Orinoco tribes, the Arawaks, and a few Caribs. Later, indentured labor from East India and China moved to the area, as did black slaves from Africa. The mission became a parish some time in the mid-nineteenth century.

Where did the image of La Divina Pastora venerated at Siparia come from? There are a number of pious legends explaining its arrival. An account written by a parish priest in the mid-nineteenth century says that, before his time, it was brought by a priest from Venezuela, who credited it with saving his life. Unfortunately, there is no written record other than this to prove or disprove the statue's origin.

Another unknown is the exact time when the image became the focus of pilgrimage, although we do know that the custom was already well established by the mid-nineteenth century. Today, the feast is celebrated in much the same way it has been traditionally, including Mass, a procession, and the rosary. Since the early 1980s, monthly devotions lead up to the feast.

And what of the Hindu celebrations at this Catholic shrine? The Hindu pilgrims begin arriving on Holy Thursday morning, along with hundreds of the very poor who come seeking alms. Vendors set up makeshift tents in the streets near the church, and a bazaar atmosphere prevails. The image of the Divina Pastora, called Sopari Mai by the Hindus, is moved into the parish hall, and devotees come in supplication and thanksgiving, bringing gifts of rice, flowers, olive oil, and coins. On Friday morning, organized pilgrimages arrive. Young babies are presented to the Holy Mother in a special ritual dance, and the hair from the first haircut of baby boys is offered to the Virgin. Alms are given to the poor who have gathered in the courtyard. Groups of Catholic volunteers serve these destitutes supper on Thursday night and a light breakfast on Friday morning.

In multicultural Trinidad, people of diverse ethnic backgrounds and other living faiths live under the Fatherhood of God. Here people of different cultures and religions have identified, in popular religiosity, with La Divina Pastora; and in a unique way, Mary is carrying out her role of Holy Shepherdess. The history of the devotion to the Good Shepherdess demonstrates that mission and evangelization must reject aggressiveness and the belittling of other religions. Here, Christians follow the directives of the Second Vatican Council in respecting others and appreciating their freedom to follow the religion of their choice. To use her image as a tool for conversion would defy what she represents to those of different faiths who come to her. Instead, La Divina Pastora provides reassurance and hope for the oppressed and leads them to God in her own way and in his own time. The focal point of popular religiosity in Trinidad, although she sits in a Roman Catholic church, the Good Shepherdess is catholic in its most universal sense.

> *The pilgrims who come here have a deep belief in the power of prayer to La Divina Pastora. With childlike simplicity they are convinced that prayer to the Madonna is a force to change matters in their lives and in the lives of others. Here, respect for the faith of others and an acceptance of the shared common values inherent in all genuine faith expressions has been pursued.*
>
> —Rev. Stephen Doyle, O.P.

Father Doyle is the parish priest of Siparia, Trinidad.

Iveron Mother of God of Montreal
Montreal, Canada

In 1982, a young Chilean convert to Orthodoxy from Canada, Jose Munoz Cortes, went to Mt. Athos on pilgrimage and acquired a modern copy of the Iveron icon of the Mother of God. On his return, the icon began to exude myrrh, which continued to flow until it was stolen. Roman Catholic, Orthodox, and even some Protestants asked to see the phenomenon and venerated the Holy Mother of God. Jose traveled the world with the icon for fifteen years until, in 1997, he was tortured and murdered. The murderers remain at large and the icon has disappeared.

Many miracles have been wrought through the Iveron Icon of the Mother of God, not only for people's bodies but first and foremost for their souls. Wherever Jose Munoz would bring the icon—whether to America or Europe, to Mt. Athos or to the Holy Land—everywhere it inspired the faithful to confess, to receive Holy Communion, to be reconciled with one another and to weep over their sins. It is a fountain of such things, of a mystical and peace-endowing grace, causing people to forget their burdens and all of their secular concerns. It is a grace which brings something akin to the joy of Pascha, the holy resurrection of Christ.

—Rev. Victor Potapov

Archpriest Victor Potapov is the rector of St. John the Baptist Russian Orthodox Cathedral in Washington, D.C.

For the complete story of this miraculous icon and the unsolved mystery of Jose Munoz's murder, please visit the special section "Other Faces of Mary" on the author's website: www.annball.com.

Koratty Muthy
Kerala, India

One of the most ancient shrines devoted to Mary in India is that of Koratty Muthy. Here Our Lady has been honored for over seven centuries by the faithful Catholics of the Syro-Malabar rite.

The Syro-Malabar community is flourishing in the church today. It is the second largest Eastern Catholic Church in the world and the major community of the ancient Thomas Christians in India. According to the tradition, St. Thomas the Apostle evangelized Malabar (today known as Kerala), the southwest coast of India.

In the late fourteenth century, Kerala was divided into

provinces ruled by feudal lords. Many Christians served in the army of one of them, Koratty Kaimal. In a battle against the rival lord, Kodassery Kartha, in 1381, the commander of Kaimal's army, Sri Kavalakkadan Kochu Vareed, was killed. There was only a single Catholic church in the area, at Ambazhakkad, and Lord Kaimal made arrangements for his commander's burial there with full military honors. Lord Karfa interfered, however, and the funeral procession began to return. When they reached Koratty, the pall bearers rested, placing the coffin on the ground. When they attempted to lift it up again, they were astonished to find that they could not lift it. When he heard of this, Lord Kaimal directed that the burial be done at that place and ordered a church to be built on the spot for his Catholic subjects. He also provided funding for the church's operation. Today, a granite cross marks the spot. Gradually, the church became known as a Marian pilgrimage center, Koratty Muthy.

Although the earliest written documents date from the eighteenth century, the tradition of the early establishment of the church is supported both by the architecture of the building and by the fact that descendents of the feudal lords still live in the area.

The image of Koratty Muthy is of the assumption type, which shows Mary holding the Child Jesus and standing on a crescent moon above a cloud with small angels. Made of ivory, it is painted primarily in gold and blue, and a large bunch of golden plantains is attached to the hem of her veil. Known as *poovankula,* the plantain is a favorite *ex voto* offering at the shrine.

A charming tradition explains why plantains are a special offering at the shrine. Many years ago, a devotee from a nearby hamlet was traveling to the shrine carrying an offering of a bunch of a special variety of plantains called *poovan pazham.* As he traveled near the town of Muringood, a rich farmer out in his fields with his laborers stopped him and asked for some of the bananas. The devotee refused, because the entire bunch was to be an offering to Our Lady.

This irritated the rich farmer, who reached over and forcibly took two bananas from the bunch and ate them.

Soon the rich man developed a stomach ache that had him writhing in pain. Doctors were called; they attempted several treatments but nothing helped. At last, they told the man that there was no sign of any disease and that the only remedy must be his repentance. The man repented, and as reparation he gave a large piece of land as an offering to Koratty Muthy. As soon as he did this, his pain vanished. The gift of plantains has been traditional at the shrine ever since. Devotees sometime take home plantains blessed at the shrine, dry and powder them, and keep the powder as a sacramental.

Two other popular legends concern places near the shrine. One is connected with the building of the Koratty Angady railway station. During one of the festivals of Koratty Muthy, a train suddenly came to a halt when it reached Koratty. All efforts to restart the train proved futile. Hearing the fireworks and drums from the festival, the passengers visited the church to venerate the image of Koratty Muthy. On their return, the train's engine started easily.

During World War II, a military air base was scheduled to be built at Koratty. In spite of the efforts at quick completion made by the contractor, no apparent progress was being made. A mysterious lady holding a young child interrupted the workers, who believed she was Koratty Muthy. The contractor gave up the plan to make a military base and erected instead the Jumna Thread Mill, which provided employment to thousands of laborers from Koratty and its suburbs. The contractor had tiny models of spades and other tools made in silver, and he presented them as an offering to Koratty Muthy. At one time, the company closed down, but it has now reopened. Devotees count this as a favor from Our Lady.

As a Marian pilgrimage center, devotees flock to the shrine throughout the year. Many give testimony of favors and blessings received from the heavenly Mother. In particular, newly wed couples come before Koratty Muthy asking her blessing on their marriage. Other devotees make a moving sight as they crawl on their knees, often with their children on their back, to ask for favors.

The annual feast of Koratty Muthy is celebrated each October on the Saturday and Sunday following the tenth of the month. From the first of the month, the faithful begin to gather, saying the rosary and praying in candlelight processions around the church. During the feast days, the image of Our Lady is taken in procession from the church to the Roopa Pura, a large open-sided building where the statue is venerated by thousands. The processions are lively, with music, drum beats, and a large, specially adorned umbrella to attract the devotees. During the festival, a novena to Koratty Muthy is prayed, and there is a daily blessing of vehicles.

The shrine was renovated, enlarged, and the new church was blessed in 1987. The interior has been refurbished with engravings, historical pictures, and relief carvings.

Heavenly Father, we adore you, we praise and thank you for your everlasting and steadfast love and for the gift of Mother Mary as our mother and protectress. We sincerely repent of our sins and humbly ask your pardon for violating our baptismal promises. O Lord, grant us spiritual, mental, and physical graces, which we beg of you through the intercession of Mother Mary, Koratty Muthy.
—Very Rev. Jose Paul Nellissery, M.A., LL.B., M.C.L.

Father Jose Paul Nellissery is the former rector of St. Mary's Forane Church, which is in the archdiocese of Ernakulam, Kerala, India.

The Sorrowful Mother

Our Lady of Siluva
Siluva, Lithuania

In 1608, Our Lady appeared to some children near the small town of Siluva, Lithuania, a rural area near a pine forest. Most of the people in the town were poor farmers, scratching out a living by tilling the soil. Older children tended the family flocks while the young ones played nearby. One summer day, the youngest children saw a woman with long hair and pretty, loose-fitting garments standing on a huge rock where they customarily played. The woman held a child in her arms, and tears were flowing from her eyes. Frightened, the children did not speak to the lady, but one boy ran to the Calvinist church to relate what they had seen.

Word of the apparition spread rapidly, and the following day a large group of people went to the site, including a Calvinist catechist and the rector of the seminary. The two churchmen upbraided the people for believing the tale of the children and said that if indeed someone did appear it must be the devil. As the catechist spoke, the woman appeared again. The frightened assembly remained silent, but the catechist gathered his courage to ask the lady why she was crying. She responded, "Formerly in this place, my Son was honored and adored, but now all that the people do is seed and cultivate the land." Having said this, the woman disappeared in the sight of everyone present.

Since the apparition was seen by a number of people, it was fruitless for the Calvinist leaders to deny it, but they continued to insist it was some trickery of the devil.

The people were confused and did not know what to believe. An old blind man in the crowd spoke up, saying, "Think what you will but I say to you that on the rock appeared not the devil, as the Calvinists would have us believe, but the Most Blessed Virgin with her Son, in whose honor once stood the old Catholic church which was destroyed many years before." This old man was adamant in his belief that an apparition had taken place.

Lithuania first accepted Catholicism in 1251, when King Mindaugas was baptized, but the faith remained dormant for two centuries because of constant wars and turmoil in the country. Vytautas the Great finally defeated the Teutonic Knights in 1410, and the faith began to spread. A pious noble, Petras Giedgaudas, built the first church in Siluva in 1457 in honor of the Nativity of the Blessed Virgin. Soon the area became a place of fervent devotion to Our Lady. When the first church burned, a new church was built, in 1500.

By the 1530s, a wave of Protestantism had swept through Europe, and a number of the Lithuanian nobles had accepted the Lutheran faith. They took possession of the church's lands. Lutheranism remained strong in the area until the middle of the sixteenth century when it gave way to Calvinism. The property was deeded to the Calvinists in 1591, and they built a church and a seminary there. It is not certain just when the Catholic church was closed; services were still being held as late as 1550. Although the nobles and upper classes had become Calvinist, the peasants and poor farmers remained faithful Catholics; but the church in Siluva was either torn down or burned by about 1570. The last pastor of the church secretly buried the treasured image of the Virgin and Child along with some other valuables and church documents in a metal-covered oak chest. He then fled for his safety, and it seemed as if Catholicism in the area was finally stamped out.

In 1588, a law was passed giving Catholics the right to repossess the churches and the property unjustly taken from them. The bishop immediately started legal proceedings to reclaim all the church property, but although he knew of the former church in Siluva, there were no documents available to a prove the claim.

In 1608, the bishop sent a representative to investigate the strange happenings in Siluva, the news of which was spreading throughout the country. When the subject of the missing documents was brought up, the blind man told how when the church was destroyed the priest had buried church treasures before fleeing to safety. Led to the area near the rock of the apparitions, the man's sight was restored. This was the first recorded miracle of Our Lady of Siluva. Falling to his knees in gratitude to God for the favor granted him, the man pointed to a place to dig for the treasure. The chest was found, and the Catholics demanded the return of the property in 1612. The legal battle lasted until 1622, when the tribunal at Vilnius decided in favor of the Catholics.

In 1624 a small wooden church was built in Siluva; but it soon proved too small for the many pilgrims who came from all over the country to view they site of the apparitions of the Mother of God, whose image was placed above the main altar. By 1629, the records indicate that more than eleven thousand faithful attended the annual feast of the Nativity celebrated in Siluva. A much larger church was consecrated in 1651, and in 1786 yet another church was built and solemnly consecrated.

Miracles and graces multiplied; and because so many faithful visited the rock on which Our Lady appeared, a chapel was built around the rock in 1663. This was replaced by a larger chapel in 1818, and a third chapel was completed in 1924. Pilgrims often approached the rock on their knees, kissing it fervently.

The earlier history of the miraculous image of Our Lady found in the hidden chest is not known, although it is possible it originated in Rome and was brought to Siluva as a gift to Petras Giedgaudas. The icon is similar to ones traditionally accredited to St. Luke. It shows the Madonna holding the Divine Infant, both attired in royal robes. When it was found after the apparitions, it was in good condition. In 1671, the many gold and silver *ex votos* that had been presented to the image were melted and used to cover the icon. Gold leaf and precious stones were also added to enhance the rich beauty of the image.

Around 1775, the bishop had a marble statue of the Virgin made in London. It was placed on the rock in the chapel and was crowned in 1886. Many of the faithful experience healing graces while praying before this image, which is known as "Health of the Sick." Later, a new statue replaced this one, which is preserved in a closed chapel in the church.

Pope Pius VI approved the cult of Our Lady of Siluva and enriched it with indulgences. On September 8th, 1786, the miraculous image was solemnly crowned in a ceremony attended by over thirty thousand people.

Sadly, in 1795, during the "Great Partition," Lithuania was taken over by Russia, who ruled the country with a heavy hand until 1904. The religious press and even the Lithuanian language were suppressed, and travel was restricted. Roads were left unpaved and became difficult to travel on, a condition that discouraged pilgrims. In the country's few years of independence, between 1918 and 1940, devotion to Our Lady of Siluva began to spread. With strength and fortitude, and in spite of Soviet oppression for over fifty years, many of the faithful continued to visit Our Lady's shrine. Pope John Paul's visit in 1993 allowed the world a glimpse of the holy site and the beautiful and miraculous image of Our Lady of Siluva.

There is an image of Our Lady of Siluva at the National Shrine of the Immaculate Conception in Washington, D.C.

At the National Shrine of the Immaculate Conception,
Washington, D.C.

On First Viewing—Our Lady of Siluva

Amazed, I see this dazzling newness
But renews the splendored sum
Of every sculptured visage
Caught in marble; softened by the message
Impressed upon your gracious image
Is the unspoken word—yet heard—supernally serene.
> For I have gazed upon you thus
> A thousand times before, a hundred ways,
> O ever "Blessed among women."
> But here I read the eternal answers
> You keep for everyman
> Who seeks a silent-strong compassion.
> Your sweet-sad eyes are placid pools
> Where unshed tears reflect your client's own.
And now I know the grand largesse
A Queen bestows
In bending with a kindly majesty
To him who pleads.
(Do you do this to keep alive the legend
That they tell of Siluva,
There soughing winds like murmured prayers
Incline the pines with swaying courtesy
Forever in your direction?)
> Oh, I forget not
> That "Salvation was laid in a Woman,"
> And that the Child you gently hold
> Is regally Divine,
> And claims with you, Divinity as kin.
> Of such a Mother and of such a Child,
> I beg the grace of patient ages
> To produce from the poor pine cones
> Of my life's Faith and Hope
> The evergreens of Charity.
> > —Sister M. Agnesine Dering, S.S.C., Ph.D.
> > Sisters of St. Casimir Chicago, Illinois

My devotion to Our Lady of Siluva began in 1991 when I visited Lithuania as it stood on the brink of freedom and independence after decades of communist oppression. I was astounded to see how the country lacked not only material things but also spiritual freedom. Yet, I found untold numbers of people who, having endured unspeakable suffering, remained deeply devoted to the faith and to Our Lady. My trip to the shrine of Siluva was in a tiny car which rocked and bounced from side to side as we slowly traveled over four miles of road strewn with rocks and purposely not paved to make the trip more difficult. Seeing the faith of many local pilgrims and the lovely statue of Our Lady holding her Child over the very rock where she appeared touched my very soul. I pray daily to Mary asking that she strengthen the faith life of all families both in Lithuania and America so that her "tears" shed on behalf of her forgotten Son in the lovely field of Siluva be not in vain. Devotion to Our Lady is the mainstay of many families in Lithuania, and I know and believe that she will assist all who invoke her assistance.

—Sister Margaret Petcavage, S.S.C.

Sister Margaret Petcavage lives in Chicago and is the vice-postulator for the beatification cause of Maria Kaupas, foundress of the Sisters of St. Casimir.

La Vulnerata
Valladolid, Spain

On September 8, 1600, Blessed Thomas Palaser, O.S.F., condemned for the crime of being a Catholic priest, was stripped, hanged, drawn, and quartered in Durham, England. At the same time in the small chapel in Valladolid, Spain, where Thomas had been ordained a scant four years before, the wife of the Catholic king of Spain was among those who welcomed a most unusual image of Our Lady to her new home at the Royal English College of St. Alban.

What was once a beautiful image of Our Lady and the Christ Child had been horribly mutilated in 1596, the year of Blessed Thomas's ordination, by the swords of English troops. They had dragged the image from its place of honor in a church in Cadiz when they overran the city. Taking the figure to the town square, they desecrated it, chopping off Our Lady's arms and slashing her face and body. All that remained of the Child were his tiny feet on his mother's knee.

When the Spaniards regained control of the city, the countess of Santa Gadea, wife of the governor of Castile, rescued the mutilated statue and gave it the place of honor in her chapel in Madrid.

During the reign of Queen Elizabeth I, Catholics in sixteenth-century England were persecuted. To be a priest was a crime; to shield them was treason. The church in the country once known as Our Lady's Dowry was watered by the blood of martyrs. It was not possible to educate priests to serve the sturdy English Catholics in their homeland, so colleges for this purpose were established elsewhere in Catholic Europe. First in the Low Countries, then in Rome at the center of the church, in France because of its proximity to England, and in Spain, under the impulse of Cardinal Allen and with the aid and direction of the Jesuits, seminaries were founded for the mission of reconverting England. King Philip II of Spain was a noted defender of the Catholic faith, and he assisted in this enterprise. In the eyes of the English monarchy, however, these colleges were hotbeds of political intrigue. "Priest hunters" sought for the graduates of the colleges when they returned to England. They were arrested, tortured, and killed.

The English college in Valladolid, Spain, was established in 1589. It was named for and put under the protection of St. Alban, the protomartyr of English Catholics in the time of Diocletian.

Established as a seminary to educate priests for the English missions, the Royal College of St. Alban, the English seminary at Valladolid, became a school of martyrs. Six saints and sixteen who have been beatified were students here before beginning their dangerous work in England. Five other graduates were also put to death for the faith in England.

In 1596, Spain was recovering from the defeat of the invincible armada and was gathering another fleet in the port of Cadiz, on its southern Atlantic coast. The earl of Essex, who together with Sir Walter Raleigh was one of England's most famous sea dogs, led an English fleet into the harbor, destroyed the Spanish fleet, and took possession of the city. English troops went on a rampage through the city. One group dragged the statue of the Virgin from her church and mutilated it in the town square.

In 1600, the staff and students of St. Alban asked the countess for the right to make spiritual reparation for their countrymen's insults to Our Lady. The wounded statue was brought to Valladolid in the carriage of Queen Margaret, surrounded with a large cortege of nobles on horseback, some Jesuits, and twenty-four students. As she passed through the streets of Valladolid, Our Lady was greeted with devotion by the townspeople who lined the streets. Here, with their own eyes, the people could see in the wounded image, not just hear in a sermon, the insults that had been heaped on Our Lady by the English. There arose among them a great swell of love, pity, and devotion, and the intention to make reparation and to pray for the conversion of those who had so grievously injured the Mother of God. For her part, Our Lady let fall a shower of favors and graces on her devotees, which they testified to by an increase in spirituality and a great number of *ex voto* offerings that enriched her cult.

The statue was installed with great solemnity in the college chapel. The bishop of Valladolid, Bartholomew de la Plaza, named the image Our Lady Vulnerata, which means "wounded" and "insulted."

From then on, generations of students stood before the statue to take a solemn vow to return to England to minister to the persecuted Catholic people of the country. During the next hundred and eighty years, twenty-seven of these were put to death in England for their faith.

Devotion to Our Lady Vulnerata increased, and in 1679 it was necessary to build a larger chapel. In 1979, marking its third centenary, the chapel was renovated, and in 1985 it was opened to the public.

Special prayers are offered weekly in reparation for the insults to Our Lady and the Child Jesus and to implore the intercession of Our Lady Vulnerata for the conversion of the people of England and Wales. The Mass of Our Lady Vulnerata is celebrated in the college by special indult on the Sunday following the feast of the Immaculate Conception.

To mark the fourth centenary of the arrival of the statue of Our Lady Vulnerata, in 2000, the statue was given a new crown, a gift from the alumni of the college, at a solemn ceremony on the feast of the Forty Martyrs of England and Wales.

Dear Mother, as I gaze on your wounded and mutilated image, I humbly beg your pardon for the grievous insults to you, great Mother of God. Help me to notice the wounded children of the world, and see your beauty in the faces of the poor and disfranchised. Let me love them better, as your Son commanded. I praise you through the faith, loyalty and blood of the missionaries who prayed for courage before your image, and I ask you to keep today's missionaries in your loving care as they, too, carry the Good News throughout the world.

Mary, Queen

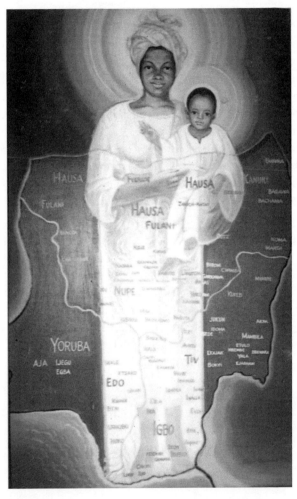

Our Lady, Queen and Protectress of Nigeria
Benin City, Nigeria

The Catholic bishops of Nigeria have declared Our Lady as patroness of the country under her title Our Lady, Queen and Protectress of Nigeria. Her feast was established for October 1. A Mass for the feast was written by a Jesuit missionary and is in use in some of the dioceses. Our Lady's feast is also Nigerian independence day, so there are many celebrations taking place in addition to the Masses in the Catholic churches and services in other churches.

Jesuits of the New York Province, assisted by Jesuits of several other provinces, have been working in Nigeria since 1962. One of the concerns of the Society of Jesus is to make the Catholic faith more real and alive wherever they serve. To help people more easily visualize Mary and her Infant Son, the Jesuit Centre in Benin City commissioned a painting of Mary, Queen and Protectress of Nigeria. The painting shows Our Lady holding the Child Jesus with his hand raised in blessing over a map of the country. Mary seems to be presenting her Son to the people and inviting them to find in him a new source of hope and unity. In traditional Nigerian clothing, the Madonna and Child are painted with black features, serenely smiling at their Nigerian people. For centuries, 250 distinct tribes occupied the country. The map in the painting shows many of the names of these tribes and indicates where they dwell. The colors of the painting symbolize the flag of the country: the map is green and Our Lady's white gown symbolizes the white stripe between the two green sides of the Nigerian flag.

For inspiration, the artist went to the people. In order to portray Our Lady, Queen and Protectress of Nigeria, and the Divine Child as real people, the artist used neighbors of the Jesuit Centre as models. At first, some people were taken aback by the painting; but once they got over the "it's never been done that way" attitude, they liked it.

The original painting hangs in the dining room of the Jesuit Centre in Benin City, a retreat house run by the order. Prayer cards and a wall calendar with the image have been made and circulated throughout the country. The image is also printed on greeting cards which have been sent worldwide.

The country of Nigeria is named for the river that runs through it. Sir Frederick Lugard delineated the boundaries in 1910. Nigeria is made up of many peoples, cultures, and ethnic groups, and each has a rich history and tradition. This wealth and variety is being brought into the praise of God in the Christian life.

North Africa carried on an active trade in commodities before the shameful era of the slave trade. Through these trade contacts, Islam and Christianity entered the country and took their place along with the country's many forms of African traditional religions.

When the first missionaries from Portugal entered the area, and from the sixteenth to the eighteenth centuries, there were a number of practices throughout the country which they sought to change: slavery, human sacrifice, the killing of twins, and polygamy. Although their efforts bore some fruit, in large part the mission efforts were not greatly successful. A second wave of missionary activity began in the nineteenth century. Liberated slaves of the Yoruba tribe enthusiastically spread Christianity. The first three Yoruba priests were ordained in 1929. Eventually, there were also massive conversions among the Igbo people. The initial evangelization in the Lower Niger region consisted of buying back slaves to free them, instructing the people to create Christian communities, and providing medical aid. Through the establishment of schools, Christianity began to take an even firmer foothold. A number of foreign religious orders made great efforts in the mission fields here. The second wave of evangelization initially attracted slaves, outcasts, the poor, and the disabled. At first, this alienated many of the other native peoples, but when some prominent people were converted, Christianity began to grow rapidly. Catechists and lay people played important roles in the spread of Catholicism. Along with the missionaries, these people showed heroic faith and endured many trials as they worked to establish the church in southern Nigeria.

The evangelization of northern Nigeria was even more difficult for a number of reasons, including the fact that Islam had been rooted in the area for so long. Although a Catholic presence was recorded in the north by the seventeenth century, and the kingdom of Kororofa at one time had nearly 100,000 Christians, foreign missionaries withdrew in frustration in the early days of the 1900s. A foothold had been established, however, and between 1930 and 1960, the time of Nigeria's political independence, other missionaries came to work alongside the dedicated laity in the ripe mission fields. The first native priests from the north were ordained in 1961.

Today the church in Nigeria is thriving. Nearly 20 percent of the population is Catholic. A local hierarchy was established in 1950, and the Catholic Bishops' Conference has emerged as an organ of unity of the local churches. Although the church in Nigeria is still young, its maturity is evident in the naming of three Nigerian Cardinals—the late Dominic Ekandem in 1976, Francis Arinze in 1985, and, most recently, Anthony Okogie in October 2003. Today's Catholics in Nigeria, living in a time of political unrest, are challenged to bear clear and united witness to their faith.

Traditionally, women in most parts of Africa have not held a high status, and this holds true in Nigeria, especially in the northern part of the country. Illiteracy, a high maternal mortality rate, high levels of domestic violence, and few legal rights are some of the problems Nigerian women face. In some tribes, when the husband dies, the woman washes his body and then drinks the water. Once his relatives learn he is dead, they come and strip the house. The woman has no recourse and must return to her family.

The human rights situation in Nigeria has become pivotal in determining the success or failure of its newly emerging democratic system. Although the country is constitutionally recognized as a secular state, its secular nature has been challenged in recent times and tensions are rising as Muslims claim a right to implement the severe *sharia* criminal legal code.

In today's Africa, the whole role and place of women is changing, and Christian missionaries have always supported the attempt to make the place of women in society more dignified and accepted, just as Christ did in his own time. The beatification of Cyprian Iwene Tansi in 1998 exemplified and highlighted the heroic witness of the Nigerian Christians and the missionaries who brought the faith to their land. In the same way, the serene black face of Our Lady, Queen and Protectress of Nigeria, exemplifies the Christian ideal of respect for all Nigerians, male and female alike.

As an expatriate living in a strange land, one of my concerns, and one of my goals, is to try and understand the people in whose country I am working. I am here as a guest, and so I work hard to learn culture, customs, music, language, and whatever will help me come to know and understand the people better. Before I can preach, I must learn the language in all its dimensions. One thing that has helped me is different images of traditional biblical and faith figures. When the painting of Our Lady, Queen and Patroness, first arrived, it was hard for some Nigerians to leave the traditional images of Our Lady that they had been raised with. I faced the same need to shift gears, but I continue to find in the faces of the mothers and children of Nigeria great hope and love and inspiration, and this image of Our Lady has become very important in that ongoing process.

—Rev. John Sheehan, S.J.

Father Sheehan is a Catholic chaplain on Kwajalein, a U.S. military base in the Republic of the Marshall Islands. He was a missionary in Nigeria for twelve years.

Our Lady of Chiquinquira
Bogota, Colombia

Under the title Our Lady of Chiquinquira, Mary is the patroness of Colombia. The image, a sixteenth-century painting, has a unique history. When it had become old, damaged, and ugly, it repaired itself.

According to the chronicles of New Spain, in 1563 Don Antonio de Santana, the Spanish chief of Sutamarchan, was especially devoted to Our Lady of the Rosary. In his private chapel he had a beautiful picture of her, which was painted by the artist Alonso de Narvaez and given to Don Antonio by a Dominican brother.

The picture was painted on a native cotton blanket. Our Lady was shown with her head slightly tilted toward her Divine Child, who was sitting on her left arm. A portrait of St. Anthony of Padua, holding a book on which the Holy Child was standing, was to the right of the Virgin. On her left side, the artist depicted St. Anthony the Apostle, along with the cross on which he was crucified.

Little by little, the cloth began to develop holes, the paint began to fade, and dirt and dust gathered on the picture until in 1578, the priest took it down from the altar. It was taken to a nearby *finca,* or ranch, belonging to Don Antonio at Chiquin-quira. Here, dirty and full of holes, with the images almost completely faded away, the blanket was used by the farm workers to carry and sort seed.

In 1585, a pious woman, Maria Ramos, a relative of Don Antonio, came to work as a domestic servant in the home of his widow on the ranch. She discovered the picture, and, on being told that it was once an image of Our Lady, she attempted to clean it, trying to remove all the dirt and grime. Although she was able to clean it, the images were almost too faded to see.

Maria made a little chapel in a hut that had been used to stable the farm's pigs. She placed the faded image of Our Lady on the wall and prayed there daily, begging the Virgin for consolation. Maria was homesick for her native land and home, and with many tears and much love she pleaded with Our Lady to make herself more visible so that she could pray better.

The chronicles of 1586 record that at about nine o'clock on the morning of December 26, a Christian Indian named Isabel was passing the door of the little hut-chapel. She was carrying her four-year-old son, Miguel, who cried out, "Mama, Mama, look at the Mother of God who is on the floor!" Isabel turned to look and saw the picture completely surrounded by a bright light that lit up the entire chapel. She called Maria Ramos at once, "Look, look, Señora, the Mother of God has come down from where she was, and it seems as if she is burning!" Maria Ramos came and realized that things were as the Indian had said, so she threw herself to her knees in front of the picture with great faith and devotion and began to pray.

Others, heeding the cries of the two women, came to see the prodigy. The picture had ignited and restored itself with beautiful colors. After a while, with much love, devotion, and respect, the picture was rehung in the same place on the wall where it had been. News of the miracle spread rapidly, and the priest came from Sutamarchan to see what had happened.

A commission was established to study the miracle, and on January 10, 1587, the archbishop of Bogota pronounced the restoration a supernatural occurrence. The fame of the picture spread throughout the country, and humble servants, working people, and Indians, as well as those of the wealthy classes, began to beg Our Lady for favors, which she granted. Twice, in times of a virulent epidemic that was killing many of the native Colombian Indians, the picture was carried out in procession and the epidemics ceased.

Through the years, there have been many miracles attributed to the intercession of Our Lady of Chiquinquira, but the one favor most granted is that of conversions. To this day, the people ask her for a change of heart for their loved ones who have lost the way, and Our Lady is credited with giving faith to thousands.

Although the painting is over four hundred years old, the colors are still bright and the images remain well defined. Pearls and jewels have been embroidered onto the picture, which is slightly over a meter in length and width.

Until her death, Maria Ramos was the main guardian of the miraculous picture of Our Lady of the Rosary of Chiquinquira. Since 1636, it has been in the custody of the Dominican Fathers. Today, the image has been proclaimed and crowned the Queen of Colombia, and Our Lady continues to attract hearts to God.

Pope Pius VII declared her patron of Colombia in 1829, and she was canonically crowned in 1919. Pope John Paul II paid homage to Our Lady of Chiquinquira when he visited Colombia in July of 1986.

> *When I was a little girl, my mother taught me to pray to the Virgin with confidence and faith. I feel her presence with me wherever I am. She has given me many graces, including one special one, in my life.*
>
> —Beatriz L. Velez-Victoria

Ms. Velez was born in Cartago, Colombia, and immigrated to the United States at the age of six. She is a merchandise assistant in advertising for Stage Stores in Houston, Texas.

Our Lady of Lebanon, Our Lady of Harissa
Harissa, Lebanon
(Replica of the Harissa monument, North Jackson, Ohio;
see also the image on page 8)

For Lebanese Catholics, the love and devotion to the Virgin Mary is like an instinct inherited from apostolic times. This devotion is the dominant note of the invincible Christianity of Lebanon, which has long suffered under persecution. As the Lebanese gaze upon Our Lady in the multitudinous shrines to her in their country, they glorify her Son and adore the divine Trinity who has exalted her.

The church of Antioch rendered a special veneration to the Mother of God in the first days of Christianity. During the seventh and eighth centuries, when many of the Eastern priests and monks fled to the West to escape the Islamic wars, many of the feasts of Mary in the Eastern churches were introduced to the West. Today, devotion to Mary is a key point in the spirituality of all Lebanese Catholics, most of whom are members of rites that came from the Antiochene tradition. In this very diversified country, love of Mary is a unifier. Not only do the Catholics and Orthodox, but also Shiites, Sunnites, and Druzes come to pray at the feet of Our Lady at her shrines.

The shrine to Our Lady of Harissa, or Our Lady of Lebanon, was begun in 1904 to commemorate the fiftieth anniversary of the proclamation of the dogma of the Immaculate Conception, a belief which the Syriac fathers, including St. Ephrem, had held to be true fifteen centuries earlier. Around the shrine and new basilica are the patriarchal residences of the Maronites and the Melchites, as well as the summer residence of the papal nuncio. Nearby is a convent of the Franciscan Fathers, and not too far away is the see of the Syriac Catholic patriarchate and the Armenian Catholic patriarchate. It is as if they have come under Our Lady's mantle to find refuge from every difficulty.

The idea for building the shrine was a joint dream of the Maronite patriarch and the papal nuncio who wanted to erect a monument to commemorate the anniversary of the dogma and show the love of Mary by the Lebanese throughout the generations. They intended a monument; it has become an international shrine for pilgrimage.

The shrine is built in the region known as "the rock" on the hill of Harissa, which overlooks the city of Jounieh, the Mediterranean Sea, and Beirut. Set in a beautiful landscape, the monument is six hundred meters above sea level. The bronze statue of the Virgin was made in Lyons, France, and is painted white. It is eight-and-one-half meters tall and stands on a stone pedestal twenty meters high. To reach the foot of the statue, pilgrims climb a spiral staircase of one hundred and four steps. The monument was erected on May 3, 1908, and Mary was proclaimed Queen of Lebanon. A feast in honor of Our Lady, Queen of Lebanon, is celebrated in Lebanon on the first Sunday of May.

During the 1954 Marian year, a statue of Mary, carved from cedar, was carried in procession across Lebanon with stational stops at 145 locations. Lifted high on arms stretched above a sea of heads, the image passed through the villages before coming to rest in the church. Each stational church tried enthusiastically to outdo the others in providing a beautiful reception for the Queen of Lebanon, and the celebration was enhanced with nocturnal vigils, confessions, and communions. Christians from all rites and people of other faiths all honored the "Saide." The verses of the Koran that celebrate the privileges of Mary were inscribed on arches of triumph. During the Marian conference in May, Cardinal Angelo Giuseppe Roncalli (later Pope John XXIII), representing Pope Pius XII, crowned the image in the presence of two hundred thousand people, proclaiming her the true Queen of Lebanon.

A replica of the Harissa monument was erected in North Jackson, Ohio, in 1963. The first Maronite bishop of the United States often commented that this project of honoring Our Lady of Lebanon in northeastern Ohio was in some special and almost unknown way a preparation for his coming and for the beginning of the first Maronite eparchy in this country. This sanctuary in honor of the Blessed Mother is cared for and supported by all Maronites and pilgrims of all religious backgrounds from every part of America. The eparchy of Our Lady of Lebanon of Los Angeles operates the national shrine. The image of Our Lady is carved from rose granite and weighs seven-and-one-half tons. It is twelve feet tall and is mounted on a four-foot pedestal set on a stone tower that is forty-two feet high. There are sixty-four steps on the spiral staircase which climbs to the top.

The image of Our Lady of Lebanon holds out her hands in invitation and love. When Lebanon was declared independent, a famous writer was asked to write a poem for the occasion. He declined, saying that what was needed was already written in the "Ya Ommallah," the hymn sung during one of the great popular devotions of Lebanon, the Benediction of Our Lady. Part of this hymn perfectly symbolizes the devotion to Our Lady of Lebanon:

> You are our Mother and our hope, our honor and our shelter. Intercede for us with your Son in order that His Mercy may take away our sins. O good and compassionate Mary, do not abandon us, but save your servants that we may be able to thank you forever and ever.

Even though Lebanon is a tiny country in the Middle East, I don't think that most are aware that there are millions of Lebanese Christians living all over the world that have maintained their Lebanese heritage. This heritage stems from their deep faith, particularly through devotion to Mary. I happen to be one of those individuals. I am a second generation Lebanese American. I did not realize the impact that Our Lady of Lebanon made on my faith until my husband and I ventured on our first trip to Lebanon a few years ago. It was a moving experience, to say the least. As we traveled from Jounieh through Beirut forward up the glorious mountain to the towns from where my grandparents migrated at the end of the nineteenth century, the visible statues and numerous shrines to Our Lady of Lebanon were overwhelming. As we approached the town of Bakfia, where the majority of my family still lives, we saw the phenomenal statue of Our Lady, who reigns atop the Maronite church overlooking miles of the most beautiful view of Lebanon down to the Mediterranean Sea. As the sun sets, a beam of light appears behind the statue that radiates her image for miles. It is an incredible sight! For me, this was a revelation that she is a major part of our way of life.

—Janice Jamail (Gemayel) Garvis

Janice is a native of Houston, Texas, and is the broker and owner of Jamail Real Estate, Inc.

Our Lady of Peking, Empress of China
Peking, China

In China, the cult of Our Lady has always emphasized reverence for Mary as Queen of Heaven and as the heavenly mother of
the individual. The beautiful picture known as Our Lady of

Peking, Empress of China, shows this high regard for the Virgin. Dressed as an empress of the Qing dynasty, she wears a long string of pearls and highly embroidered, traditional lotus shoes. The Child Jesus is robed as an imperial prince. The Virgin tenderly holds her Child close to her with her left arm. The heavenly prince gestures with both hands toward his mother as if beckoning the viewer to come to her protective heart.

Around the turn of the century, Monsignor Alphonse Favier, vicar apostolic of Peking, had a chapel erected in the church of Beitang in honor of Our Lady of Deliverance, represented as the Empress of China. The painting and chapel were given in gratitude for Our Lady's help in a terrible siege against the Christians during the summer of 1900.

Although there is evidence that Alopen, a Syrian monk, brought Christianity to China in the seventh century, it was a Franciscan, John of Montecorvino, who came to Beijing in the last years of the eleventh century and began missionary activity there. Pope Clement V gave him pastoral authority over the whole of China and the Far East. He built at least two churches and made several thousand converts; but after his death the church fell into oblivion and was not reestablished until Jesuit Father Matteo Ricci arrived in the first days of the fifteenth century. Through the efforts of Ricci and his companions, the faith took root and began to spread to other parts of the country. In the four centuries since Ricci's time, the church in China has passed through both good and bad times. There have been periods of freedom and years of persecution. Since the founding of the People's Republic in 1949, a new period of persecution of Catholics in China began; and with the Cultural Revolution (1966–1976) many symbols of religion were destroyed. The Catholic church in China was driven underground.

Near the end of the nineteenth century, China was one of the largest fields for apostolic labor, and priests of the Congregation of the Mission, known as Lazarists in Europe and Vincentians in North America, were in charge of the important mission of Peking, as well as of several other apostolic vicariates. No strangers to persecution and violence, they came to China at the close of the eighteenth century. Two of their own, St. Francis Regis Clet in 1820 and St. Jean-Gabriel Perboyre in 1840, gave their lives as martyrs and have been canonized; others spilled their blood as seed, and the apostolic work continued.

Another period of persecution began during the Boxer rebellion, which affected many of the areas where the Vincentians labored.

The Boxers were members of two of the secret societies that have long flourished in China. Claiming supernatural powers, they championed the national spirit against foreigners. The real ruler of China at this time was Empress Dowager, and she encouraged the Boxers in their uprising. Though Christian missionaries were not the real cause of the uprising, its horrors fell most heavily on them, partly because many were living exposed among the people while other foreigners lived in better protected areas. The slaughter began first in the rural areas. Over six thousand Chinese Catholics were killed.

On May 30, 1900, Vincentian father Claude Guilloux wrote from the mission at Peking to his superior at Paray-le-Monial, France:

> We live in constant terror, but we are more concerned for our dear neophytes than for ourselves. Already, many Christians have been massacred, and a great number of villages burned. . . . In general, our beloved neophytes manifest great courage, which has been sustained by remarkable proofs of divine favor. In several places, during the combat with the Boxers, the pagans themselves saw the Blessed Virgin in the middle of the Christians; and during the massacre of a Christian settlement, the pagans heard a heavenly music and they understood that the victims were happy. Finally, two evenings ago, ten Christian guards of an establishment much in danger at the gates of Pekin, saw during the night a large white cross which they venerated.

At last, the fury of the Boxers turned toward Peking. In the early part of June, 1900, Pe Tang was besieged by thousands of Boxers, reinforced by soldiers from the regular army. The siege lasted from June to August, yet the missionaries, and most of the eighty Europeans and over three thousand Chinese Catholics with them, the majority of whom were women and children, were spared. Four hundred were killed by bullets, in explosions, or died from starvation or disease and were buried; more than fifty others, mostly children, were killed in explosions, and no remains could be found to bury. Toward the end of the siege, food was reduced to two ounces a day per person, and the people were reduced to eating leaves and grass.

The missionary center of the Vincentians in Beijing was in the Northern Cathedral (now Beitang, formerly called Pei-t'ang or Pe-Tang). It was founded in the year 1693, when the Chinese imperial government still regarded Christianity favorably. It is dedicated to Jesus the Savior and was transferred to the Vincentians after the Jesuits were disbanded. Built in Gothic style, it remains the largest church in China. Today's church was built in 1890 by the French mission, and it was formerly the center of a large complex of schools, homes for orphans, and hospitals. The buildings were in a spacious and strongly walled compound. After the siege, hundreds of bullet and shell holes in the roofs and walls and pits from mine explosions gave mute testimony to the fury of the attack.

In 1901, Bishop Favier, a burly, bearded man in his mid-sixties, wrote to his superiors in France: "It is already a marvelous event this defense of Petang and its 1,400 meters of walls by forty French and Italian seamen, without guns, against five or six thousand fanatical Chinese aided by powerful artillery." He continued by pointing out that the vigilance and skill of their leader, Lieutenant Paul Henry, and the heroism shown by the sailors were not enough to explain two months of victorious resistance against the relentless attacks. Every night, the Chinese had directed heavy gunfire at the roofs of the cathedral and its balustrades, but there was no one there to defend the cathedral. After the liberation, the

Chinese themselves provided the solution to the mystery. "How is it," they said, "that you did not see anything? Every night, a white Lady walked along the roof, and the balustrade was lined with white soldiers with wings."

Bishop Favier's votive chapel was in the new church that today belongs to the Chinese Catholic Patriotic Association and has been the center of the diocese since 1959. The church was reoccupied in 1976 and restored in 1985. The association is not in communion with Rome. The lovely image of Our Lady of Peking remains on display here.

Of China's estimated eleven million Catholics, just over half belong to the clandestine, or underground, church, which is faithful to Rome. Driven underground, the church in China patiently waits in hope for another period of religious freedom.

I always think of the Virgin Mary as the heavenly mother of all mankind. She has played an important role in my life. Since I left my parents' home in China for America sixteen years ago, mother Mary has always been with me. She looks over me from Heaven above, listens to my prayers, gives me strength and courage, and I can always find comfort and security in her. Mother Mary's love for me and for all people inspires me everyday to love others with great patience and a forgiving heart, which is a difficult craft that needs more than one lifetime to master. One of the ways my family shows our love to mother Mary is to say the rosary every evening.

—Theresa Zheng Attaldo

Theresa Zheng Attaldo is a Chinese-American Catholic. She and her husband, Jim, live in New York.

Selected Bibliography

In addition to the items listed below, I have relied heavily on printed information and personal contacts with many people throughout the world.

Anonymous. *Annals of the Congregation of the Mission.* Vol. 7, no. 1. Emmitsburg, Md.: Congregation of the Mission, 1900.

——. *Ladyewell, Past and Present.* Preston, Lancastershire: Shrine, undated.

——. *Ligeros Datos Historicos de la Aparicion de la Divina Infantita.* Leon, Mexico: Missioneros de la Natividad de Maria, undated.

——. *Notre Dame du Guiaudet.* Lanrivain: Church of Guiaudet, undated.

——. *Our Lady of the Garden.* Rome: Gianelli Editions, 1981.

——. *Resumen Historico de los Missioneros de la Natividad de Maria.* Leon, Mexico: Missioneros de la Natividad de Maria, undated.

——. *Santa Maria la Real de Nájera.* Nájera, Spain: Monastery of Nájera, undated.

——. "Siluva, First Apparition in Europe." *Journeys* 17, no. 1 (Spring 2003).

——. "Thousands Venerate Relic of St. Juan Diego as National Tour Begins." *The Texas Catholic Herald* (January 13, 2003): 6.

Attwater, Donald. *A Dictionary of Mary.* New York: P. J. Kennedy and Sons, 1956.

Ball, Ann. *A Litany of Mary.* Huntington, Ind.: Our Sunday Visitor, 1985.

Boyea, Earl. *Gabriel Richard, Servant of God.* Detroit: St. Anne de Detroit, 2000.

Boyuer, Marie-France. *The Cult of the Virgin.* New York: Thames and Hudson, 2000.

Bunson, Matthew, ed. *Encyclopedia of Saints.* Huntington, Ind.: Our Sunday Visitor, 2003.

Brankin, Patrick. *Bilingual Ritual of Hispanic Popular Catholicism.* New Hope, Ky.: New Hope Publications, 2002.

Buela, P. Carlos. *Novena en honor a la Virgen de Chapi.* Arequipa, Peru: Monjas del Monasterio del Nino Dios, 1997.

Burrieza Sanchez, Javier. *Una Isla de Inglaterra en Castilla.* Valladolid: Iglesia del Real Colegio de San Albano, 2000.

Bussard, Paul. *Marian Shrines in the Holyland.* St. Paul, Minn.: Catholic Digest, 1959.

Bussard, Paul. *St. John's Cathedral in Holland.* St. Paul, Minn.: Catholic Digest, 1959.

Chidgey, Paul. *Our Lady of Penrhys.* Welsh Province: Catholic Truth Society, 1962.

DEA Student Publication. *The Aetas of Subic Bay.* Waterville, Vt.: Stan Chop, 1992.

Domas, Anna Wurtz. *Mary U.S.A.* Huntington, Ind.: Our Sunday Visitor, 1979.

Dunstan, Richard. "Brothers and Sisters from the East," in *Our Sunday Visitor,* February 9, 2003, p. 12.

Healy, Thomas. *Our Lady of Aberdeen, The Hidden Statue.* Glasgow: John S. Burns and Sons, 1976.

Kovalchuk, Feodor S. *Wonderworking Icons of the Theotokos.* Youngstown, Oh.: Catholic Publishing Company, 1985.

Noel, Theresa. *A Short History of La Divina Pastora Parish, Siparia.* Siparia: La Divina Pastora Parish, undated.

O'Carroll, Michael, C.S.Sp. *Theotokos: A Theological Encyclopedia of the Blessed Virgin Mary.* Wilmington, Del.: Michael Glazier, 1982.

O'Conner, Kathryn Stoner. *Presidio LaBahia.* Austin, Tex.: Von Beckmann-Jones Co., 1966.

Peters, Louis. *Mary in the Calendar of the Maronite Church.* St. Louis: St. Raymond Maronite Church, 1990.

Reilly, Leo, C.S.B. *Ste. Anne de Detroit.* Detroit: Ste. Anne de Detroit, 2001.

Salesman, Eliecer. *El Libro de la Virgen.* Bogota: Ediciones Salesiana, 1992.

Shelton, James. "A Catholic Encounter in China," in *Our Sunday Visitor,* September 7, 1986, p. 10.

Thornton, Francis, ed. *Marian Shrines in the Holyland.* St. Paul, Minn.: Catholic Digest, 1959.

Varghese, Roy Abraham. *God-sent: A History of the Accredited Apparitions of Mary.* New York: Crossroad Publishing Company, 2000.

Weiser, Francis X. *Handbook of Christian Feasts and Customs.* New York: Harcourt Brace and World, 1958.

Yla, Stasys. "The First Apparition of the Mother of God in Europe," in *Lithuanian American News Journal,* May 1998.

Zayek, Francis. *Mary, Cedar of Our Catholic Faith.* Detroit: Diocese of St. Maron, 1975.

Thank You

I thank those without whom I could not have written this book: those who sent art, information, and comments on the various titles of Our Lady, and those whose friendship, prayers, and help assisted me. If I have failed to thank anyone by name, Our Blessed Mother will extend her special blessing to them.

Hazel Alphonse, Castries, St. Lucia
Rev. Anthony Anderson, SOLT, Juarez, Mexico
Sister Inez Aparicio, Staten Island, New York
Brother Edwin Arteaga, Rome, Italy
Joanna Ball, Gulfport, Mississippi
Alejandro Bermudez, Lima, Peru
Marzina Bernez, Germany
Chuck Bolton, Miami, Florida
Javier Burrieza-Sanchez, Valladolid, Spain
Carlos Cabral, Miami, Florida
Carmen Chapa, Alice, Texas
Sister Alda Civiera, R.S.C.J., Aberdeen, Scotland
Daniel Chidgey, Cardiff, Wales
Canon Paul Chidgey, Herfordshire, England
Sister Mary Christine, O.P., Newark, New Jersey
Marge Craven, Huntington, Massachusetts
Professor Bary Cunliffe, Oxford, England
Czech Heritage Society of Houston
Rev. Valentine de Sousa, S.J., Tokyo, Japan
Julie Douglas, Jacksonville, Texas
Rev. Stephen Doyle, O.P., Siparia, Trinidad
Sister Dorothy Dwyer, Tampa, Florida
Al Ewer, Sugar Land, Texas
Mel Francis, Houston, Texas

Loretta Gallagher, Newbury Port, Massachusetts
Patrick Galliou, Brittany, France
Michelle Ghio, Malta
Rev. John Giuliana, West Redding, Connecticut
Pere Augustin Goujon, Brittany, France
Brother J. Nicholas Grahmann, F.S.C., Santa Fe, New Mexico
Professor Patrick J. Hayes, Quincy, Illinois
Ms. Janis Jamail, Houston, Texas
Susan Kerr, Austin, Texas
Leo Knowles, Manchester, England
Anna Krpec, Houston, Texas
Father Campion Lally, Tokyo, Japan
Rev. John Thomas Lane, S.S.S., Albuquerque, New Mexico
Mrs. Elizabeth Law, San Francisco, California
Monica Llerena, Van Nuys, California
Morgan Macintosh, Chicago, Illinois
Very Rev. Gregory Mansour, St. Louis, Missouri
Rev. Jose Marcone, La Pintaus, Chile
Sister Andrea Margarita, La Huerta, Philippines
Mike Marshall, St. Francis, South Dakota
Msgr. Patrick McCormick, Fresno, California
Rev. Anthony McGuire, Washington, D.C.
Sandra Miesel, Indianapolis, Indiana
Karin Murthough, Houston, Texas
Rev. Jose Paul Nellissery, Kerala, India
Rev. Donald Noiseux, Huntington, Massachusetts
Rev. Vince O'Malley, C.M., Emmitsburg, Maryland
Rev. Ivan Page, M. Afr., Rome, Italy
Rev. John J. Paul, S.J., Bronx, New York
Sister Margaret Petcavage, S.S.C., Chicago, Illinois
Phan van Dung, Houston, Texas
Archpriest Victor Potapov, Washington, D.C.
Rev. Bob Power, C.S.B., Las Cruces, New Mexico
Provinzialat der Kapuziner, Vienna, Austria
Harold Rennie, Halifax, Nova Scotia
Burt Richards, Norwich, England

Rev. Walter Rossi, Washington, D.C.
Michelle Rubio, Goliad, Texas
Sister Marie Rutland, O.P., Newark, New Jersey
Sister Mary Lawrence Scanlan, O.S.F., Allegany, New York
Maria Ruiz Scaperlandia, Norman, Oklahoma
Rev. Tom Sepulveda, C.S.B., Detroit, Michigan
Thomas J. Serafin, Los Angeles, California
Rev. John Sheehan, Lagos, Nigeria
Michael Skelly, Edinburgh, Scotland
Sister Alzbeta Soudkova, Czech Republic
Darlene Sunnerton, Huronia, Ontario, Canada
Mary Talamini, Houston, Texas
Susan Tassone, Chicago, Illinois
Tzer Lee Thao, Fresno, California
Canon Etienne Van Billoen, Brussels, Belgium
Pieter Van Den Bos, The Hague, Netherlands
Father J.B. Nguyen Van Them, S.D.B. Provincial, St. John Bosco,
    Vietnam Province
Frank Varga, Del Ray Beach, Florida
Roy Varghese, Garland, Texas
Bebe Velez, Houston, Texas
Debbie Wang, Corpus Christi, Texas
Mr. Newton Warzecha, Goliad, Texas
Bea Whitfil, Houston, Texas
Rev. Chue Ying Vang, Washington, D.C.
Rev. Fausto Zelaya, California
Theresa Zheng, New York
Ed Zych, Hohenwald, Tennessee